Vex Aleron

Defying Tradition for LGBTQ Equality in Kaevin – Unauthorized

Dmitri Jiang

ISBN: 9781779697806
Imprint: Telephasic Workshop
Copyright © 2024 Dmitri Jiang.
All Rights Reserved.

Contents

Introduction   **1**
The Early Years   1
Awakening Activism   12

Bibliography   **21**
The Path to Leadership   26
Facing Backlash and Resistance   38

Bibliography   **43**

Chapter 2   **51**
Pushing Boundaries   51
Love, Relationships, and Activism   64

Bibliography   **77**
International Influence   77
The Price of Activism   89

Bibliography   **93**

Chapter 3   **103**
Political Engagement   103
Taking on the Media   116

Bibliography   **125**
Building Bridges   128
Activism in the Digital Age   140

Chapter 4   **153**

Intersectionality in LGBTQ Activism 153
Legacy and Future 165

Bibliography 175
The Power of Art and Creativity 178

Bibliography 191

Index 193

Introduction

The Early Years

Growing up in a Traditional Society

In the quaint town of Kaevin, where the rolling hills meet the horizon and the sun casts a golden hue over the cobblestone streets, Vex Aleron's journey began amidst the echoes of tradition and the weight of expectation. Growing up in a traditional society often means navigating a complex web of cultural norms and familial expectations, where conformity is prized above individuality. This environment can be particularly challenging for those who find themselves on the fringes of societal norms, especially within the LGBTQ community.

The Cultural Landscape

The cultural landscape of Kaevin was deeply rooted in conservative values, where gender roles were rigidly defined, and deviations from the norm were met with skepticism or outright hostility. Traditional beliefs often dictated not only how one should behave but also how one should identify. The expectation was clear: to grow up, marry, and follow a well-trodden path laid out by generations before. In this context, Vex's burgeoning awareness of their identity felt like an act of rebellion—a whisper of authenticity in a cacophony of conformity.

Theoretical Framework

To understand Vex's experience, one can draw upon the *Social Identity Theory*, which posits that a person's sense of who they are is based on their group membership(s). In a traditional society, the dominant group often defines the standards of identity, leaving those who identify differently to grapple with internalized stigma and external pressure. This theory elucidates the struggles faced by LGBTQ individuals in environments that prioritize heteronormativity, as they navigate a landscape fraught with potential ostracization.

Navigating Identity

As a child, Vex found solace in the quiet corners of their imagination, where they could explore identities that felt true to their essence. However, the reality of growing up in a traditional society meant that these explorations were often shadowed by fear. The fear of being discovered, the fear of rejection, and the fear of being labeled as "different" loomed large. This internal conflict is not uncommon; many LGBTQ individuals experience a sense of cognitive dissonance, where their self-perception clashes with societal expectations.

For instance, consider the case of a young boy in Kaevin who enjoys ballet. In a traditional society, such an interest might be met with ridicule or disdain, pushing him to suppress his passion in favor of more "acceptable" pursuits. This societal pressure can lead to a phenomenon known as *internalized homophobia*, where individuals adopt the negative beliefs of their society towards their own identities. Such experiences can have profound impacts on mental health, leading to anxiety, depression, and a pervasive sense of isolation.

Finding Support

Despite the challenges, Vex was fortunate to find support in unexpected places. A teacher, who recognized the signs of struggle in Vex's demeanor, became a beacon of hope. This educator introduced Vex to literature that celebrated diversity and inclusivity, allowing them to see reflections of their own experiences in the stories of others. This exposure was transformative; it provided Vex with a sense of belonging and the realization that they were not alone in their journey.

Research indicates that supportive relationships can significantly mitigate the negative effects of growing up in a traditional society. For LGBTQ youth, having at least one affirming adult can reduce the risk of mental health issues and increase resilience. Vex's experience exemplifies this theory, as the encouragement from their teacher fostered a sense of empowerment that would later fuel their activism.

The Impact of Family Dynamics

The family dynamic also played a crucial role in shaping Vex's identity. In a traditional household, discussions around sexuality and gender identity were often taboo. Vex's parents, while loving, held firmly to conventional beliefs, which created a chasm between their expectations and Vex's emerging identity. The internal struggle of wanting to be true to oneself while also seeking parental approval is a common narrative among LGBTQ youth.

One poignant example of this conflict is when Vex attempted to express their identity during a family gathering. The conversation turned to marriage and children, and Vex felt a wave of anxiety wash over them. The fear of disappointing their parents loomed large, leading to a decision to remain silent. This moment encapsulated the broader struggle faced by many LGBTQ individuals: the desire for acceptance clashing with the need for authenticity.

Conclusion

Growing up in a traditional society is a complex interplay of identity, culture, and familial expectations. For Vex Aleron, the journey was marked by challenges that shaped their understanding of self and the world around them. The experience of navigating a traditional landscape, fraught with societal pressures and expectations, laid the groundwork for Vex's eventual awakening as an activist. It was through the struggles of youth that the seeds of resilience and determination were planted, ultimately leading to a life dedicated to advocating for LGBTQ equality in Kaevin and beyond.

In this way, Vex's early years serve not only as a personal narrative but also as a reflection of the broader LGBTQ experience in traditional societies, highlighting the importance of support, understanding, and the courage to embrace one's true self against the tide of convention.

Discovering a Different Identity

The journey of self-discovery is often a complex and multifaceted process, particularly for individuals within the LGBTQ community. For Vex Aleron, this journey began in the confines of a traditional society that upheld rigid norms regarding gender and sexuality. Growing up in Kaevin, Vex was exposed to a culture that celebrated heteronormativity, often at the expense of those who dared to deviate from the expected path.

The Struggle with Self-Identity

As Vex navigated the early years of adolescence, the internal conflict between societal expectations and personal truths became increasingly palpable. Theories of identity development, such as Erik Erikson's stages of psychosocial development, suggest that individuals grapple with identity versus role confusion during the teenage years [?]. For Vex, this stage was marked by confusion and fear, as the desire to conform clashed with an emerging sense of self that felt distinctly different from the norm.

The Role of Language and Labels

Language plays a crucial role in identity formation. The absence of appropriate terminology can hinder one's ability to articulate their experiences and feelings. Vex found solace in the discovery of LGBTQ-specific language that provided a framework to understand and express their identity. Terms such as "queer" and "non-binary" became lifelines, offering a sense of belonging and validation. As Judith Butler posits in her theory of gender performativity, identity is not merely a fixed state but rather a series of performances shaped by societal expectations and personal agency [?].

Cultural and Familial Influences

Cultural background and familial expectations significantly impact the process of identity discovery. In Vex's case, family dynamics played a pivotal role. The pressure to conform to traditional gender roles was palpable, with familial expectations often manifesting as a source of anxiety and fear. The concept of "familial rejection" is well-documented in LGBTQ studies, highlighting the emotional toll it takes on individuals who come out to unsupportive families [?].

Vex's initial attempts to discuss their feelings with family members were met with confusion and resistance, leading to a profound sense of isolation. This experience is not uncommon; many LGBTQ individuals report feelings of alienation when their identities clash with familial beliefs.

Finding Community and Support

In the face of adversity, Vex sought refuge in unexpected places. The discovery of online communities and support groups became a turning point. Platforms such as Tumblr and Reddit provided a space for Vex to connect with others who shared similar experiences, fostering a sense of community that transcended geographical boundaries. The importance of community in identity formation is underscored by the concept of "chosen family," which refers to the social networks that individuals create outside of their biological families [?].

Through these online interactions, Vex began to embrace their identity more fully, participating in discussions that challenged societal norms and explored the nuances of queer existence. This newfound sense of belonging was instrumental in helping Vex articulate their identity, leading to a more profound understanding of self.

The Intersection of Identity and Activism

As Vex's understanding of their identity deepened, so too did their awareness of the broader struggles faced by the LGBTQ community. The intersectionality theory, as proposed by Kimberlé Crenshaw, emphasizes the interconnected nature of social categorizations such as race, class, and gender, and how these intersections create unique experiences of oppression [4]. Vex began to recognize how their own identity as a queer individual intersected with other social identities, leading to a commitment to activism that sought to address these multifaceted issues.

This realization marked the beginning of Vex's journey toward activism, as they began to understand that their personal struggles were part of a larger narrative. The decision to embrace a different identity not only empowered Vex on a personal level but also ignited a passion for advocating for change within their community.

Conclusion

Discovering a different identity is a transformative experience that shapes individuals in profound ways. For Vex Aleron, this journey was marked by challenges, revelations, and ultimately, empowerment. The interplay between personal identity and societal expectations created a rich tapestry of experiences that would inform Vex's future activism. As they continued to navigate the complexities of their identity, Vex emerged not only as an individual but as a beacon of hope for others on similar journeys, illustrating the power of authenticity in the fight for LGBTQ equality.

Navigating High School as a Queer Teen

High school is often characterized as a formative period in a young person's life, rife with challenges and opportunities for growth. For queer teens, this phase can be particularly tumultuous, as they grapple with their identities amidst a backdrop of societal expectations and peer dynamics. The experience of navigating high school as a queer teen is not merely a personal journey; it is a complex interplay of identity, acceptance, and resilience.

The Social Landscape

The social environment of high school can be both a sanctuary and a battleground for queer teens. Many students are still in the process of discovering their own identities, leading to a climate where conformity often reigns supreme. According to [?], high school culture frequently emphasizes heteronormativity, which can alienate those who do not fit within these narrow definitions. The pressure to conform can result in significant internal conflict, as queer teens may feel compelled to hide their true selves to gain acceptance.

Identity Formation

Identity formation during adolescence is crucial, as theorized by Erik Erikson in his stages of psychosocial development. In the fifth stage, *Identity vs. Role Confusion*, teens explore various identities, which can be particularly challenging for queer youth. Many queer teens face the dilemma of reconciling their sexual orientation or gender identity with societal norms. The process of self-acceptance can be fraught with anxiety, as external validation from peers and family often feels necessary for self-worth.

$$\text{Self-Acceptance} = \text{Authenticity} + \text{Support} - \text{Rejection} \qquad (1)$$

This equation illustrates that self-acceptance is enhanced by authenticity and support while diminished by rejection. In high school, where social circles can be unforgiving, the stakes are high. The fear of rejection from friends, family, and peers can lead to a reluctance to come out, resulting in a phenomenon known as *closeting*.

Experiences of Bullying and Discrimination

The journey of queer teens in high school is often marred by experiences of bullying and discrimination. Studies indicate that LGBTQ+ students are at a higher risk of being bullied compared to their heterosexual peers, with up to 70% reporting harassment based on their sexual orientation or gender identity [?]. This harassment can take many forms, from verbal taunts to physical violence, contributing to a hostile school environment.

The impact of bullying can be profound, leading to mental health issues such as anxiety, depression, and suicidal ideation. The *National School Climate Survey* found that queer teens who experience bullying are more likely to report lower academic performance and higher rates of absenteeism [?]. This underscores the importance of supportive school environments where diversity is celebrated, rather than stigmatized.

Finding Community

Despite the challenges, many queer teens find solace in community. Supportive friends, LGBTQ+ clubs, and online forums can provide safe spaces for self-expression and connection. The establishment of Gay-Straight Alliances (GSAs) in schools has been instrumental in fostering inclusivity and providing resources for queer youth. According to research by [?], participation in GSAs is associated with lower levels of victimization and higher levels of self-esteem among LGBTQ+ students.

Additionally, queer teens often seek out role models and representation in media. The visibility of LGBTQ+ characters in television and film can help normalize queer identities and provide hope for young people grappling with their own identities. For instance, shows like *Euphoria* and *Sex Education* highlight the complexities of queer adolescence, offering both affirmation and understanding.

The Role of Educators

Educators play a pivotal role in shaping the experiences of queer teens in high school. Inclusive curricula that reflect diverse identities can foster a sense of belonging and validation. Training for teachers on LGBTQ+ issues can also mitigate instances of discrimination and bullying. According to a study by [?], schools with LGBTQ+-inclusive policies report a more positive climate for all students, leading to better academic outcomes and overall well-being.

Conclusion

Navigating high school as a queer teen is a multifaceted experience marked by both challenges and triumphs. The journey toward self-acceptance is often complicated by societal pressures, bullying, and the quest for community. However, with supportive peers, inclusive environments, and the guidance of empathetic educators, queer teens can find their voices and carve out spaces where they can thrive. The resilience developed during these formative years not only shapes their identities but also lays the groundwork for future activism and advocacy in the fight for LGBTQ+ equality.

Finding Support in Unexpected Places

In the journey of self-discovery, individuals often find support in the most surprising places. For Vex Aleron, this was no different. Growing up in a traditional society where conformity was the norm, Vex initially felt isolated in their quest for identity. However, as they navigated the complexities of adolescence, unexpected sources of support began to emerge, illuminating a path towards acceptance and empowerment.

One of the most significant sources of support came from the unlikeliest of allies: a group of older students who were members of the Student Alliance for Equality (SAE). This organization, initially perceived as a fringe group within the school, became a beacon of hope for Vex. The SAE was founded on principles of inclusivity and advocacy, aiming to create a safe space for all students, regardless of their sexual orientation or gender identity. The older students, who had faced their own struggles, became mentors to Vex, providing not only guidance but also a sense of belonging that had been previously elusive.

$$\text{Support} = f(\text{Community Engagement, Mentorship, Shared Experiences}) \quad (2)$$

This equation illustrates the multifaceted nature of support, where community engagement, mentorship, and shared experiences intertwine to create a nurturing environment. Vex's involvement with the SAE allowed them to engage with peers who understood the nuances of being queer in a traditional setting. The mentorship provided by older members equipped Vex with the tools necessary to navigate high school dynamics, empowering them to articulate their identity confidently.

In addition to peer support, Vex found encouragement from an unexpected source: a history teacher who recognized the struggles faced by LGBTQ students. This teacher, Ms. Thompson, had a reputation for being unconventional, often incorporating discussions about social justice and equality into her curriculum. During a lesson on civil rights movements, she introduced the topic of LGBTQ rights, prompting Vex to share their experiences. The response was overwhelmingly positive; Ms. Thompson not only validated Vex's feelings but also encouraged them to express their identity through art and writing.

$$\text{Teacher Support} = \text{Empathy} + \text{Validation} + \text{Encouragement} \quad (3)$$

This equation emphasizes the critical role educators play in fostering a supportive environment. Ms. Thompson's empathetic approach, validation of Vex's experiences, and encouragement to explore their identity through creative outlets significantly impacted Vex's self-acceptance. Such support from educators can often be a game-changer, especially in environments where familial acceptance is lacking.

Moreover, Vex discovered a community within the local library, where they attended a weekly book club focused on LGBTQ literature. This gathering

THE EARLY YEARS

attracted a diverse group of individuals, ranging from allies to those exploring their own identities. The discussions were rich and enlightening, allowing Vex to see reflections of their own struggles in the stories of others. The library, often viewed as a quiet place for study, transformed into a sanctuary of understanding and acceptance.

$$\text{Community} = \text{Diversity} + \text{Shared Narratives} + \text{Support Systems} \quad (4)$$

Here, the equation illustrates how community is built on diversity, shared narratives, and robust support systems. By engaging with others who shared similar experiences, Vex learned the power of storytelling as a means of connection and healing. This book club not only provided a platform for discussion but also fostered friendships that transcended the boundaries of sexual orientation and gender identity.

Through these unexpected channels of support, Vex began to cultivate resilience. They learned that while traditional structures might not provide the acceptance they sought, alternative avenues could offer the same, if not greater, validation. This realization was pivotal, as it instilled in Vex the understanding that support often comes from those who have navigated similar paths, regardless of their backgrounds.

In reflecting on this period of their life, Vex recognized that finding support in unexpected places was not merely a stroke of luck but rather a testament to the importance of seeking out and fostering connections within one's community. This experience laid the groundwork for Vex's future activism, as they became determined to create spaces where others could find the same support they had discovered.

Ultimately, Vex's journey highlighted a critical aspect of LGBTQ activism: the need for inclusive and supportive environments that recognize the diverse experiences of individuals. By sharing their story, Vex aimed to inspire others to seek support in unconventional places, emphasizing that community is often found where one least expects it.

$$\text{Empowerment} = \text{Support} + \text{Resilience} + \text{Community Engagement} \quad (5)$$

This final equation encapsulates the essence of Vex's experiences. Empowerment is a product of the support received, the resilience built through challenges, and active engagement within the community. As Vex continued their journey, these foundational elements would serve as guiding principles in their fight for LGBTQ equality in Kaevin and beyond.

Coming Out to Family and Friends

Coming out is often regarded as one of the most significant milestones in the life of an LGBTQ individual. It represents a transition from a life of concealment to one of authenticity and openness. For Vex Aleron, this moment was both exhilarating and terrifying, a duality that many in the LGBTQ community can relate to.

The Emotional Landscape

The process of coming out can be fraught with a myriad of emotions, ranging from fear and anxiety to relief and joy. Research indicates that the fear of rejection or negative responses from loved ones often leads to a phenomenon known as *anticipatory anxiety*, which can significantly impact mental health (Meyer, 2003). Vex experienced this firsthand, grappling with the potential fallout of revealing his true self to those closest to him.

Theoretical Frameworks

To understand the complexities of coming out, we can reference *Cass's Model of Sexual Identity Formation*, which outlines several stages individuals may go through during this process. These stages include:

- **Identity Confusion:** The initial stage where individuals question their sexual orientation.

- **Identity Comparison:** Acknowledging feelings of attraction but feeling isolated.

- **Identity Tolerance:** Accepting one's identity while still fearing societal rejection.

- **Identity Acceptance:** Embracing one's identity and seeking out community.

- **Identity Pride:** Taking pride in one's sexual orientation and becoming more public about it.

- **Identity Synthesis:** Integrating one's sexual identity into the broader spectrum of self.

Vex found himself navigating through these stages, often oscillating between pride and fear as he prepared to come out.

The Coming Out Process

Vex chose a quiet evening to come out to his family. The setting was intimate, with soft lighting and the comforting aroma of his mother's cooking wafting through the air. This environment, however, did little to quell his racing heart. He recalled the moment vividly:

> "I sat at the dinner table, my fork hovering over my plate, and I felt the weight of the world on my shoulders. I knew that this moment could change everything."

He began by expressing gratitude for their support throughout his life, a tactic often recommended by LGBTQ advocates to soften the initial impact of the revelation. As he uttered the words, "I'm gay," he felt a rush of vulnerability wash over him.

Reactions and Consequences

The reactions from family members can vary widely, and Vex's experience was no exception. His mother responded with tears, not of disappointment, but of confusion and concern for her son's future. His father, on the other hand, was silent, a stark contrast to the emotional outpouring of his mother.

Research shows that family acceptance is crucial for the well-being of LGBTQ youth. According to the Family Acceptance Project, individuals with supportive families are significantly less likely to experience depression and suicidal ideation (Ryan et al., 2009). Vex's experience mirrored this; while his father's silence was disheartening, his mother's support became a lifeline.

Friendships and Community Support

Following his family, Vex faced the task of coming out to friends. This was a different landscape altogether, one marked by the camaraderie and shared experiences of youth. He opted for a more casual approach, inviting friends over for a movie night.

As the credits rolled, he took a deep breath and said, "There's something I need to share with you all." The initial shock was palpable, but soon laughter and support filled the room. One friend exclaimed, "We love you, Vex! You're still the same person!" This reaction highlighted the importance of chosen family within the LGBTQ community, a concept that Vex would come to cherish.

Navigating Challenges

However, not all experiences were positive. Vex faced challenges with some friends who struggled to accept his identity. This led to a painful realization about the fluidity of relationships and the necessity of surrounding oneself with supportive individuals.

The concept of *social support* is crucial here; it has been shown that positive social interactions can mitigate the effects of stress and enhance resilience (Cohen & Wills, 1985). Vex learned to prioritize friendships that uplifted him and distanced himself from those that did not.

Reflections on the Journey

Coming out was not a one-time event for Vex but rather an ongoing journey. Each interaction, whether with family or friends, shaped his understanding of himself and his place in the world. He often reflected on the words of LGBTQ activist Harvey Milk: "You gotta give 'em hope." Vex realized that by coming out, he was not just affirming his identity but also paving the way for others to do the same.

In conclusion, Vex Aleron's coming out experience illustrates the intricate dance of vulnerability, fear, and liberation. It serves as a reminder that while the path may be fraught with challenges, the journey toward authenticity is a powerful act of courage, one that can inspire others to embrace their true selves.

Awakening Activism

Discovering LGBTQ Activism

Vex Aleron's journey into LGBTQ activism began as a spark ignited by personal experiences and societal injustices. Growing up in Kaevin, a region steeped in traditional values and norms, Vex felt the weight of conformity pressing down on him. However, as he navigated the tumultuous waters of adolescence, he began to discover a vibrant community of activists fighting for LGBTQ rights. This discovery was not merely a personal revelation; it was a call to action that would shape the trajectory of his life.

Theoretical Framework

To understand the emergence of LGBTQ activism, one can reference the *Social Movement Theory*, which posits that social movements arise in response to perceived injustices. According to Tilly (2004), social movements are collective challenges to elites, authorities, or cultural norms. Vex's awakening to activism can be seen as a reaction to the systemic inequalities faced by LGBTQ individuals in his community.

Furthermore, the *Queer Theory* framework offers insight into the nature of identity and resistance. Queer Theory, as articulated by scholars like Judith Butler and Michel Foucault, challenges the binary understanding of gender and sexuality, advocating for a more fluid conception of identity. Vex's journey was influenced by these theoretical underpinnings, allowing him to embrace his identity and challenge the societal norms that sought to suppress it.

Initial Encounters with Activism

Vex's first encounter with LGBTQ activism occurred during a local high school assembly where a guest speaker, a prominent LGBTQ activist, shared their story of struggle and resilience. The speaker's words resonated deeply with Vex, illuminating the possibilities of advocacy and community engagement. This moment marked a pivotal point in his life, igniting a desire to not only understand but actively participate in the fight for equality.

Inspired, Vex sought out local LGBTQ organizations and attended community meetings. Here, he met like-minded individuals who shared their stories of hardship and triumph. These interactions were instrumental in shaping Vex's understanding of the broader LGBTQ rights movement, highlighting the importance of solidarity and collective action.

Challenges Faced

Despite the excitement of discovering activism, Vex encountered significant challenges. One of the primary obstacles was the pervasive culture of homophobia that permeated his school and community. Vex faced backlash from peers who viewed his growing involvement in activism as a threat to traditional values. This hostility manifested in various forms, from verbal harassment to social ostracism.

Moreover, the lack of representation and resources for LGBTQ youth in Kaevin posed a significant barrier. Many organizations were underfunded and struggled to reach marginalized communities. Vex recognized that for activism to be effective, it needed to be inclusive and accessible, addressing the unique challenges faced by LGBTQ individuals, particularly those from diverse backgrounds.

The Role of Education

Education played a crucial role in Vex's discovery of activism. He immersed himself in literature on LGBTQ history, rights, and theory. Books such as *The Gay Revolution: The Story of the Struggle* by Lillian Faderman and *Queer (In)Justice: The Criminalization of LGBT People in the United States* by Joey L. Mogul, Andrea J. Ritchie, and Kay Whitlock provided Vex with a historical context for the struggles faced by LGBTQ individuals.

This educational journey not only equipped Vex with knowledge but also empowered him to articulate the issues at stake. He began to engage in discussions with peers, challenging misconceptions and advocating for a more inclusive understanding of identity.

Mobilizing for Change

As Vex's understanding of LGBTQ activism deepened, he became increasingly involved in mobilizing efforts within his school. He organized awareness campaigns, workshops, and discussions aimed at fostering a more inclusive environment. One notable event was a "Day of Silence," where students were encouraged to refrain from speaking to honor those who had lost their lives to anti-LGBTQ violence. This event garnered significant attention and served as a catalyst for broader discussions on LGBTQ rights within the school.

Vex also recognized the importance of allyship. He reached out to straight allies, encouraging them to stand in solidarity with the LGBTQ community. By fostering an environment of understanding and support, Vex aimed to create a more inclusive space for all students.

Conclusion

The discovery of LGBTQ activism was a transformative experience for Vex Aleron. It was a journey marked by personal growth, resilience, and a commitment to social justice. Through education, community engagement, and mobilization, Vex began to carve out a space for himself and others in the fight for equality. This awakening not only shaped his identity but also laid the foundation for his future endeavors as a prominent activist in Kaevin.

As Vex continued to navigate the complexities of activism, he understood that the path ahead would be fraught with challenges. However, armed with knowledge, community support, and an unwavering commitment to justice, he was ready to embrace the fight for LGBTQ rights with open arms.

Joining the Student Alliance for Equality

In the bustling hallways of Kaevin High, where the echoes of laughter mingled with whispers of tradition, Vex Aleron found a sanctuary in the Student Alliance for Equality (SAE). This organization, a beacon of hope for many marginalized voices, was not just a club; it was a movement, a collective of passionate individuals united by a singular purpose: to advocate for LGBTQ rights and foster an inclusive environment within the school and beyond.

Vex's decision to join SAE was not merely a personal choice; it was a strategic pivot in their journey toward activism. The theoretical framework of social movements, as articulated by Charles Tilly, posits that collective action arises from shared grievances and a desire for social change. Vex recognized that their own struggles with identity and acceptance were part of a larger narrative that demanded attention. The SAE provided a platform where these grievances could be articulated and addressed, transforming individual pain into collective power.

Upon joining, Vex was immediately struck by the diversity of the group. Members hailed from various backgrounds, each bringing unique perspectives shaped by their experiences. This intersectionality, as highlighted by Kimberlé Crenshaw, was crucial in understanding the multifaceted nature of oppression. The SAE was not solely focused on sexual orientation; it also embraced issues related to race, gender, and socioeconomic status, creating a rich tapestry of voices advocating for equality.

The initial meetings were electric with energy and enthusiasm. Vex quickly learned about the historical context of LGBTQ activism, particularly in Kaevin. The region had a tumultuous past regarding LGBTQ rights, with numerous instances of discrimination and violence. The group's mission was clear: to educate the student body, challenge harmful stereotypes, and create a safe space for all students. Vex recalled the words of Harvey Milk, who famously said, "Hope will never be silent." This mantra resonated deeply within the SAE, inspiring members to amplify their voices in the face of adversity.

However, joining the SAE was not without its challenges. The group faced significant opposition from conservative factions within the school community. This resistance manifested in various forms, from derogatory comments in the hallways to organized protests against SAE events. Vex and their peers understood that they were not just fighting for their rights; they were also confronting deeply ingrained societal norms that resisted change. The work of sociologist Erving Goffman on stigma illuminated the complexities of this struggle, as Vex grappled with the duality of being both a student and an activist.

One of the first initiatives Vex participated in was the "Know Your Rights" campaign, aimed at educating students about their legal protections against discrimination. This initiative was grounded in the belief that knowledge is power. By equipping students with information, the SAE aimed to empower them to stand up against injustices they might face. Vex organized workshops that included guest speakers—local activists, legal experts, and even allies from the faculty—who shared their insights and experiences. The turnout was overwhelming, with students eager to learn and engage in discussions about their rights and the importance of allyship.

As Vex became more involved, they also took on a leadership role within the SAE, coordinating events that highlighted LGBTQ history and culture. One such event was the "Pride Week" celebration, which included a series of workshops, film screenings, and guest lectures. This initiative not only celebrated LGBTQ identities but also fostered a sense of belonging among students. The success of Pride Week was a testament to the power of community organizing and the effectiveness of grassroots activism, echoing the sentiments of Saul Alinsky, who emphasized the importance of building relationships to effect change.

Despite the triumphs, Vex faced moments of self-doubt and fear. The weight of responsibility was heavy, and the potential for backlash loomed large. Yet, the support from fellow SAE members provided a safety net, reinforcing the notion that activism is not a solitary endeavor. The solidarity within the group was a powerful reminder of the strength found in unity, a theme often echoed in the writings of Audre Lorde, who asserted that "we are not meant to be alone."

In summary, Vex's journey in joining the Student Alliance for Equality marked a pivotal moment in their life. It was a transformative experience that not only deepened their understanding of LGBTQ issues but also ignited a passion for activism that would shape their future endeavors. The SAE became a microcosm of the broader LGBTQ rights movement, where theory met practice, and individual stories converged into a powerful collective narrative. Through this involvement, Vex learned that the fight for equality is not just about changing laws; it is about changing hearts and minds, one conversation at a time.

Protesting for LGBTQ Rights

Protesting for LGBTQ rights has been a cornerstone of the movement's struggle for equality and acceptance. It is through these protests that voices are amplified, narratives are reshaped, and societal norms are challenged. In the context of Kaevin, Vex Aleron emerged as a pivotal figure in this fight, galvanizing peers and allies to take a stand against systemic discrimination and social injustice.

Theoretical Framework

The protests for LGBTQ rights can be understood through various theoretical lenses, including social movement theory, which posits that collective action arises from shared grievances and a desire for social change. According to Tilly (2004), social movements are characterized by their ability to mobilize individuals around a common cause, leveraging resources, and creating networks of solidarity. This framework is essential in understanding how Vex and their peers organized protests in Kaevin.

Furthermore, the concept of intersectionality, introduced by Crenshaw (1989), plays a critical role in shaping LGBTQ activism. It highlights how various social identities—such as race, gender, and class—interact with one another, influencing individuals' experiences of oppression. Vex recognized that the fight for LGBTQ rights must also address these intersecting identities to create a more inclusive movement.

The Call to Action

In the early days of Vex's activism, the landscape in Kaevin was marred by discriminatory policies and pervasive homophobia. The need for a visible and vocal protest became increasingly urgent. Vex, alongside the Student Alliance for Equality, organized their first protest, which aimed to challenge the local government's refusal to recognize LGBTQ rights.

The protest was meticulously planned, emphasizing non-violent resistance inspired by historical figures such as Martin Luther King Jr. and Harvey Milk. Vex utilized social media platforms to spread the word, creating a digital flyer that read:

> "*Love is Love: March for Equality!*"

The event was designed not only to raise awareness but also to foster a sense of community among LGBTQ individuals and allies.

Challenges Faced

However, organizing such protests was not without its challenges. Vex and their team faced significant opposition from conservative groups and individuals who viewed the protest as a threat to traditional values. In the weeks leading up to the event, Vex received threatening messages, highlighting the risks associated with being a visible activist.

Despite these threats, the determination to protest remained steadfast. Vex understood that the visibility of LGBTQ individuals was crucial in challenging stereotypes and dismantling prejudice. As noted by Gamson (1995), visibility can serve as a powerful tool in social movements, as it humanizes the struggle and fosters empathy among the broader population.

The Protest Day

On the day of the protest, Vex and their supporters gathered at the town square, armed with colorful banners, signs, and a palpable sense of purpose. The atmosphere was electric, with chants of "Equal rights for all!" echoing through the streets. It was a moment of solidarity, showcasing the diversity within the LGBTQ community.

The protest featured speeches from various activists, including local leaders and allies, who shared personal stories of discrimination and resilience. Vex delivered a passionate speech, emphasizing the importance of unity and the need for systemic change:

> "We are here today not just for ourselves, but for those who came before us and those who will come after us. Our fight is for love, acceptance, and equality!"

Impact and Recognition

The protest garnered significant media attention, drawing coverage from local news outlets and social media platforms. This visibility helped to elevate the conversation around LGBTQ rights in Kaevin, challenging the status quo and prompting discussions among community members.

In the aftermath, Vex and the Student Alliance for Equality received recognition from various organizations, marking a turning point in their activism. The protest not only raised awareness but also inspired other youth to engage in activism, creating a ripple effect throughout the community.

As noted by Della Porta and Diani (2006), successful protests can lead to increased mobilization and the establishment of new networks, which was evident in the growth of LGBTQ organizations in Kaevin following the event.

Conclusion

Protesting for LGBTQ rights is not merely an act of defiance; it is a declaration of existence and a demand for justice. Vex Aleron's journey in organizing protests highlights the power of collective action in the face of adversity. Through protests, individuals can assert their rights, challenge societal norms, and ultimately pave the way for a more inclusive and equitable future.

The lessons learned from these protests continue to resonate, reminding us that the fight for LGBTQ rights is an ongoing journey that requires courage, resilience, and unwavering solidarity.

Bibliography

[1] Tilly, C. (2004). *Social Movements, 1768-2004.* Paradigm Publishers.

[2] Crenshaw, K. (1989). Demarginalizing the Intersection of Race and Sex: A Black Feminist Critique of Antidiscrimination Doctrine, Feminist Theory and Antiracist Politics. *University of Chicago Legal Forum*, 1989(1), 139-167.

[3] Gamson, J. (1995). *Must Identity Movements Self-Destruct? A Queer Dilemma.* In *The Politics of Gay Rights* (pp. 197-218). University of Chicago Press.

[4] Della Porta, D., & Diani, M. (2006). *Social Movements: An Introduction.* Blackwell Publishing.

The Battle for Equal Rights in Kaevin

In the heart of Kaevin, a quiet revolution was brewing. Vex Aleron, a young queer activist, was about to embark on a journey that would challenge the very fabric of a society steeped in traditional values. The battle for equal rights in Kaevin was not merely a political struggle; it was a fight for dignity, recognition, and the right to love freely. As Vex stepped onto this path, they were armed with passion, resilience, and a deep understanding of the theories that underpinned their activism.

Theoretical Frameworks

At the core of Vex's activism was the understanding of intersectionality, a term coined by Kimberlé Crenshaw in 1989. Intersectionality posits that individuals experience overlapping social identities, which can lead to unique forms of discrimination and privilege. In the context of LGBTQ rights, this theory illuminated the complexities faced by queer individuals in Kaevin, particularly those who also identified as people of color, disabled, or from marginalized socioeconomic backgrounds.

Vex's strategy was informed by the work of scholars like Judith Butler, who argued that gender and sexual identities are performative and socially constructed. This perspective empowered Vex to challenge the rigid norms that dictated what it meant to be queer in Kaevin, advocating for a more fluid understanding of identity that embraced diversity.

The Problems at Hand

The battle for equal rights in Kaevin was fraught with challenges. The societal landscape was marred by deep-seated homophobia and transphobia, often perpetuated by misinformation and stereotypes. For instance, many residents believed that homosexuality was a phase or a moral failing, a misconception that Vex and their allies sought to dismantle through education and outreach.

Moreover, Kaevin's legal framework offered scant protections for LGBTQ individuals. Discrimination in employment, housing, and healthcare was rampant, leaving many vulnerable to abuse and marginalization. Vex often cited the statistic that LGBTQ youth were five times more likely to experience homelessness than their heterosexual peers, a sobering reality that galvanized their activism.

Mobilizing the Community

Recognizing the need for collective action, Vex began mobilizing the community. They organized workshops to educate their peers about LGBTQ issues and the importance of allyship. The slogan, "Love is a Right, Not a Privilege," became a rallying cry for the movement, encapsulating the essence of their struggle.

Vex also reached out to local organizations, forming alliances with groups that focused on racial justice, women's rights, and disability advocacy. This coalition-building was crucial, as it highlighted the interconnectedness of various social justice movements. Together, they organized community forums where residents could share their experiences and discuss solutions to the pervasive discrimination faced by LGBTQ individuals.

Protests and Demonstrations

The culmination of Vex's efforts was the organization of a series of protests demanding equal rights. The first of these protests, dubbed "Kaevin Stands for Equality," drew hundreds of participants. Armed with colorful banners and a fierce determination, they marched through the streets, chanting slogans that echoed their demands for justice.

One particularly poignant moment occurred when a group of parents joined the march, holding signs that read "We Love Our LGBTQ Children." This display of support was a turning point, as it challenged the narrative that LGBTQ identities were something to be ashamed of. It sent a powerful message to the community that love and acceptance could transcend societal prejudices.

Confronting Opposition

As the movement gained momentum, it inevitably faced backlash. Conservative groups began to mobilize, framing LGBTQ rights as a threat to traditional family values. They launched campaigns filled with misinformation, claiming that allowing same-sex marriage would lead to the collapse of society. Vex countered these narratives by emphasizing the importance of love and commitment, arguing that families come in many forms and that all families deserve legal recognition and protection.

The tension reached a boiling point when a local religious leader publicly condemned the movement, calling for a "return to traditional values." In response, Vex and their allies organized a counter-demonstration, emphasizing the need for dialogue and understanding. They invited members of the religious community to participate in discussions, fostering a space where differing viewpoints could be expressed respectfully.

Legislative Advocacy

Recognizing that protests alone would not secure the rights they sought, Vex turned their attention to legislative advocacy. They began meeting with local politicians, sharing personal stories that humanized the struggle for LGBTQ rights. Vex understood that policy change required not only passion but also strategic engagement with those in power.

Through persistent lobbying, Vex and their allies managed to draft a bill aimed at prohibiting discrimination based on sexual orientation and gender identity in housing and employment. The process was arduous, filled with setbacks and moments of doubt. However, Vex's unwavering commitment inspired many to join the cause, leading to a groundswell of support that could not be ignored.

A Turning Point

The turning point in the battle for equal rights in Kaevin came when the bill was finally brought to a vote. The atmosphere was electric, with supporters gathering outside the legislative building, holding signs and chanting for justice. Vex stood at the forefront, embodying the hopes and dreams of countless individuals who had fought for recognition and dignity.

When the vote was announced, the room erupted into cheers as the bill passed. It was a moment of triumph, not just for Vex but for the entire LGBTQ community in Kaevin. This victory was a testament to the power of grassroots activism and the importance of standing together in the face of adversity.

Reflecting on the Battle

The battle for equal rights in Kaevin was far from over, but Vex's efforts had laid a strong foundation for future activism. They understood that change takes time, and while the passage of the bill was a significant milestone, it was only the beginning. Vex continued to advocate for comprehensive LGBTQ education in schools, mental health resources for queer youth, and ongoing support for marginalized voices within the community.

In reflecting on their journey, Vex often quoted the civil rights leader Martin Luther King Jr., stating, "Injustice anywhere is a threat to justice everywhere." This sentiment encapsulated their belief that the fight for LGBTQ rights was not just about personal freedom; it was about creating a more just and equitable society for all.

The battle for equal rights in Kaevin was a testament to the power of resilience, community, and love. Through their tireless efforts, Vex Aleron had not only changed the narrative around LGBTQ identities in their hometown but had also inspired a new generation of activists to continue the fight for equality.

Gaining Recognition as a Young Activist

As Vex Aleron embarked on their journey of activism, gaining recognition as a young activist became both a personal goal and a societal necessity. In a world where the voices of youth are often marginalized, Vex's rise to prominence was not just a matter of visibility but a profound statement about the power of youth in the fight for LGBTQ rights.

The Importance of Youth Voices

Young activists play a crucial role in social movements; they bring fresh perspectives, unyielding passion, and a unique understanding of the challenges facing their generation. Theories of youth activism suggest that engagement in social issues at a young age fosters a lifelong commitment to advocacy. According to [?], youth activism is characterized by its ability to challenge the status quo, often employing innovative strategies that resonate with their peers.

Building a Platform

Vex's initial recognition came from their ability to articulate the struggles faced by LGBTQ youth in Kaevin. By leveraging social media platforms, Vex shared personal stories and experiences that resonated with many. This digital presence was not merely a tool for self-expression but a strategic move to build a community of supporters. The use of hashtags, such as #KaevinPride and #YouthForEquality, allowed Vex to connect with like-minded individuals across the globe.

$$\text{Engagement} = \frac{\text{Content Quality} \times \text{Frequency of Posts}}{\text{Negative Feedback}} \quad (6)$$

This equation illustrates that the level of engagement Vex received was directly proportional to the quality of their content and the frequency of their posts, while inversely related to the negative feedback encountered. Vex's ability to navigate this landscape was pivotal in transforming their personal narrative into a collective movement.

Recognition through Activism

As Vex became more involved in the Student Alliance for Equality, their efforts did not go unnoticed. The organization recognized the potential in Vex's leadership and appointed them as a spokesperson for various campaigns. This role provided Vex with a platform to advocate for LGBTQ rights on a larger scale, including organizing workshops and seminars aimed at educating peers about inclusivity and acceptance.

One notable campaign led by Vex was the "Voices of Kaevin" initiative, which aimed to highlight the stories of LGBTQ individuals within the community. This initiative not only amplified marginalized voices but also garnered media attention, further solidifying Vex's status as a prominent activist. The campaign was successful in part due to its strategic engagement with local media outlets and influencers, creating a ripple effect that spread awareness beyond the immediate community.

Challenges and Setbacks

However, the path to recognition was fraught with challenges. Vex faced backlash from conservative factions within Kaevin, who perceived their activism as a threat to traditional values. This resistance manifested in various forms, including online harassment and public protests against LGBTQ rights initiatives.

Despite these obstacles, Vex's resilience shone through. They utilized these experiences to fuel their activism, often addressing the issues of backlash in public forums and discussions. Vex articulated a clear message: adversity is not a deterrent but a catalyst for change. This perspective resonated with many young activists, further enhancing Vex's reputation as a determined and fearless leader.

The Role of Allies

Allies also played a significant role in Vex's recognition as an activist. Support from both LGBTQ individuals and their straight allies helped to amplify Vex's voice. Collaborative efforts with local businesses, educational institutions, and community organizations created a network of support that was essential for the success of various initiatives.

The importance of allyship in activism is well-documented; allies can leverage their privilege to advocate for marginalized communities, thus broadening the reach and impact of social movements. Vex's ability to foster these relationships was instrumental in their rise to prominence, illustrating the power of unity in activism.

Conclusion

In summary, Vex Aleron's journey toward recognition as a young activist was marked by strategic engagement, resilience in the face of adversity, and the cultivation of supportive networks. Their story exemplifies the potential of youth activism to effect change and challenge societal norms. As Vex continues to inspire others, their recognition serves as a beacon of hope for young activists everywhere, reminding them that their voices matter and that they have the power to shape the future.

The Path to Leadership

Running for Student Council President

The journey to becoming the Student Council President at Kaevin High School was not just a personal ambition for Vex Aleron; it was a bold statement against the traditional norms that had long dictated the social landscape of the institution. Vex recognized that the role of Student Council President could serve as a powerful platform to advocate for LGBTQ rights and inclusivity within the school community.

The Decision to Run

The decision to run for president was fueled by a combination of personal experience and a desire for change. Vex had witnessed firsthand the struggles faced by LGBTQ students, from bullying to exclusion in school activities. The realization that leadership could be a vehicle for change became a pivotal moment in Vex's life. This decision was not without its challenges. Vex faced the daunting task of overcoming the stigma associated with being openly queer in a traditional society, where conservative values often overshadowed progressive ideas.

Campaign Strategy

Vex's campaign strategy was rooted in authenticity and connection. The first step was to build a diverse coalition of supporters. Vex reached out to allies across various student groups, including the LGBTQ Alliance, the Environmental Club, and even the Sports Teams, emphasizing that inclusivity benefits everyone. This approach was grounded in the theory of *intersectionality*, which posits that overlapping social identities—such as race, gender, and sexual orientation—can create unique modes of discrimination and privilege [?].

The campaign slogan, *"Unity in Diversity"*, encapsulated Vex's vision. This slogan was not merely a catchy phrase; it was a call to action that resonated deeply with the student body, encouraging them to embrace their differences as strengths.

Challenges and Opposition

Running for president was not without its obstacles. Vex faced significant opposition from a faction of students who believed that a queer individual should not lead the council. This group, often characterized by a rigid adherence to traditional values, launched a campaign of misinformation, attempting to discredit Vex's qualifications and intentions.

One notable instance involved a rumor that Vex intended to implement a "gay agenda" that would undermine the values of the school. This claim was not only unfounded but also highlighted the pervasive ignorance about LGBTQ issues. To counteract this, Vex organized a series of open forums where students could voice their concerns and ask questions directly. These forums utilized the principles of *dialogic communication*, fostering an environment where dialogue could replace divisive rhetoric [?].

Implementing LGBTQ-Inclusive Policies

Vex's platform included a commitment to LGBTQ-inclusive policies, which would ensure that all students felt represented and safe within the school environment. This included proposals for the implementation of anti-bullying programs specifically addressing homophobia and transphobia, as well as the establishment of a Gender and Sexuality Alliance (GSA).

The theoretical framework of *social justice education* informed these proposals, which emphasized the need for educational institutions to actively promote equity and inclusion [?]. Vex argued that the Student Council should not only represent the student body but also serve as a catalyst for change, ensuring that every voice was heard.

Engaging the Student Body

To engage the student body, Vex utilized both traditional campaigning methods and innovative approaches. Flyers and posters were plastered across the school, but Vex also took to social media platforms to reach a broader audience. This dual strategy was grounded in the concept of *multimodal communication*, recognizing that diverse communication channels are essential for effective outreach [?].

Vex hosted events that celebrated diversity, such as a "Culture and Pride Day," where students could share their backgrounds and experiences. This initiative not only fostered community spirit but also highlighted the importance of representation.

The Election Outcome

On the day of the election, the atmosphere in the school was electric. Vex delivered a heartfelt speech that emphasized unity, love, and the importance of standing up for one another. The outcome was a testament to the power of resilience and community support. Vex was elected Student Council President, marking a significant milestone not only for Vex but also for the LGBTQ community at Kaevin High School.

The victory was celebrated as a triumph over adversity and a step toward a more inclusive environment. Vex's leadership would go on to inspire other students to embrace their identities and advocate for change, proving that representation matters.

Conclusion

Running for Student Council President was more than just a personal achievement for Vex Aleron; it was a transformative experience that reshaped the narrative around LGBTQ representation in Kaevin. Through strategic campaigning, community engagement, and a commitment to inclusivity, Vex not only secured a leadership position but also laid the groundwork for future activism within the school.

This chapter in Vex's life serves as a reminder that challenging the status quo is not only possible but necessary for progress. It underscores the importance of representation and the role that young leaders play in advocating for equality and acceptance in their communities.

Overcoming Challenges and Opposition

In the journey of activism, particularly within the LGBTQ community, the path to leadership is often fraught with challenges and opposition. For Vex Aleron, this phase of their activism was not merely a test of resolve but a crucible that shaped their identity as a leader.

One of the foremost challenges Vex faced was the entrenched opposition from traditionalist factions within their school and community. This opposition was often rooted in deeply held beliefs about gender and sexuality, which manifested in both overt and covert resistance. Vex's determination to run for Student Council President was met with skepticism and hostility, particularly from those who viewed their candidacy as a threat to the status quo.

Navigating Hostile Environments

To navigate these hostile environments, Vex employed a strategy of engagement and dialogue. They understood that confronting opposition head-on could lead to further entrenchment of prejudices. Instead, Vex focused on building relationships with peers who were undecided or neutral. This approach is supported by social identity theory, which posits that individuals are more likely to change their views when they feel a sense of belonging and connection with others (Tajfel & Turner, 1986).

Through informal discussions and organized forums, Vex created spaces for open dialogue. They invited both supporters and skeptics to share their views, fostering an environment where people felt heard. This not only diffused some of the tension but also allowed Vex to present their vision for a more inclusive school environment.

Resilience Against Personal Attacks

As Vex's visibility grew, so did the personal attacks against them. Online harassment became a new battlefield, with derogatory comments and threats surfacing on social media platforms. The psychological impact of such attacks can be profound, leading to feelings of isolation and anxiety. However, Vex's resilience shone through as they sought support from their community. They organized workshops focusing on mental health and coping strategies for LGBTQ youth, emphasizing the importance of collective strength in the face of adversity.

The concept of resilience in the face of opposition is well-documented in psychological literature. According to Masten (2001), resilience is not just an individual trait but a dynamic process that can be fostered through supportive relationships and community engagement. Vex's ability to rally support from friends, mentors, and allies exemplified this dynamic process, reinforcing their resolve to continue advocating for LGBTQ rights.

Countering Misinformation

One of the most insidious forms of opposition came in the shape of misinformation. Vex and their allies faced numerous instances where false narratives about LGBTQ individuals were propagated, often fueled by fear and misunderstanding. To counter this, Vex initiated an awareness campaign that focused on educating their peers about LGBTQ issues, rights, and the realities of being queer in a traditional society.

Utilizing social media as a platform, Vex shared personal stories, statistics, and educational resources. The effectiveness of this approach is supported by the Elaboration Likelihood Model (Petty & Cacioppo, 1986), which suggests that individuals are more likely to be persuaded by messages that are personally relevant and well-structured. By connecting with their audience on an emotional level, Vex was able to shift perceptions and dispel harmful myths.

Building Alliances

Recognizing that they could not face these challenges alone, Vex actively sought to build alliances with other marginalized groups within the school. This coalition-building was essential in amplifying their voice and creating a united front against opposition. By collaborating with organizations representing racial minorities, women, and other marginalized communities, Vex demonstrated that the fight for equality was interconnected.

The concept of intersectionality, introduced by Kimberlé Crenshaw (1989), emphasizes the importance of recognizing how various forms of oppression intersect. Vex's ability to weave together the narratives of different groups not only strengthened their position but also fostered a sense of solidarity that transcended individual struggles.

Conclusion

In summary, overcoming challenges and opposition is a critical aspect of Vex Aleron's journey as a young activist. Through strategic engagement, resilience, countering misinformation, and building alliances, Vex not only navigated the turbulent waters of activism but also emerged as a formidable leader. Their experiences serve as a testament to the power of perseverance and the importance of community in the ongoing fight for LGBTQ rights in Kaevin and beyond. The lessons learned during this phase of their activism would lay the groundwork for future endeavors, reinforcing the belief that true change is possible when individuals come together in solidarity.

Implementing LGBTQ-Inclusive Policies

Implementing LGBTQ-inclusive policies is a critical step in advancing equality and ensuring that all individuals, regardless of their sexual orientation or gender identity, feel safe and valued in educational institutions. This section will explore the theoretical frameworks underpinning such policies, the challenges faced during implementation, and notable examples that illustrate successful strategies.

Theoretical Frameworks

At the heart of LGBTQ-inclusive policy implementation is the recognition of intersectionality, a concept introduced by Kimberlé Crenshaw. Intersectionality posits that individuals experience overlapping systems of discrimination and privilege based on various aspects of their identity, including race, gender, sexuality, and socio-economic status. This framework is essential for developing comprehensive policies that address the unique challenges faced by LGBTQ individuals, particularly those who also belong to marginalized racial or ethnic groups.

Furthermore, the Social Ecological Model (SEM) offers a multi-layered approach to understanding the various influences on LGBTQ individuals' experiences. The SEM encompasses five levels: individual, relationship, community, societal, and policy. By addressing these levels, policymakers can create a more holistic and effective approach to fostering an inclusive environment.

Challenges in Implementation

Despite the theoretical underpinnings, implementing LGBTQ-inclusive policies often encounters significant obstacles:

- **Resistance from Stakeholders:** Many educational institutions face pushback from parents, community members, and even staff who may hold conservative views on LGBTQ issues. This resistance can manifest as protests, petitions, or even legal challenges aimed at reversing inclusive policies.

- **Lack of Awareness and Training:** A common barrier is the lack of awareness and understanding of LGBTQ issues among educators and administrators. Without proper training, staff may inadvertently perpetuate discrimination or fail to support LGBTQ students adequately.

- **Insufficient Resources:** Implementing inclusive policies often requires financial and human resources that many institutions may not have. This can limit the development of training programs, support services, and educational materials that promote LGBTQ inclusion.

- **Policy Fragmentation:** In many cases, policies aimed at promoting LGBTQ inclusion are not cohesive or comprehensive. Fragmented policies can lead to gaps in protection, leaving some individuals vulnerable to discrimination or harassment.

Successful Examples

Despite these challenges, several institutions have successfully implemented LGBTQ-inclusive policies, serving as models for others to follow. Notable examples include:

- **University of California System:** The University of California system has made significant strides in LGBTQ inclusion by establishing a comprehensive set of policies that address non-discrimination, housing, healthcare, and support services for LGBTQ students. Their commitment to training staff and faculty on LGBTQ issues has fostered a more inclusive campus environment.

- **The Massachusetts Safe Schools Program:** This program provides resources and training for schools to create safe and supportive environments for LGBTQ students. It includes a focus on anti-bullying policies and the integration of LGBTQ topics into the curriculum, ensuring that all students receive an education that reflects diverse identities.

- **The New York City Department of Education:** NYC's Department of Education has implemented a policy requiring all schools to create LGBTQ-inclusive curricula. This initiative not only promotes understanding and acceptance among students but also empowers LGBTQ youth by affirming their identities in the educational context.

- **The Trevor Project:** While not an educational institution, The Trevor Project has been instrumental in advocating for LGBTQ-inclusive policies across schools nationwide. Their resources, including training for educators and crisis intervention services, have helped to inform and shape inclusive practices in numerous districts.

Evaluating Policy Impact

To ensure the effectiveness of LGBTQ-inclusive policies, it is crucial to establish evaluation mechanisms. These mechanisms can include:

- **Surveys and Feedback:** Regular surveys of students, parents, and staff can provide insights into the perceptions of inclusivity within the institution. Feedback mechanisms allow for the continuous improvement of policies based on the experiences of the community.

- **Data Collection:** Collecting data on incidents of discrimination, bullying, and harassment can help institutions assess the impact of their policies. Analyzing trends over time can inform future policy adjustments and resource allocation.

- **Partnerships with LGBTQ Organizations:** Collaborating with local and national LGBTQ organizations can provide valuable expertise and resources for evaluating the effectiveness of policies. These partnerships can also help institutions stay informed about best practices and emerging issues within the LGBTQ community.

In conclusion, implementing LGBTQ-inclusive policies is an essential component of fostering an equitable and supportive environment for all students.

By utilizing theoretical frameworks, addressing challenges, learning from successful examples, and establishing evaluation mechanisms, educational institutions can make significant strides toward inclusivity. The journey toward equality is ongoing, but with commitment and collaboration, it is possible to create spaces where every individual can thrive.

Boosting LGBTQ Visibility on Campus

In the heart of Kaevin's educational landscape, Vex Aleron recognized that boosting LGBTQ visibility was not merely a matter of representation but a crucial step toward fostering an inclusive environment for all students. The visibility of LGBTQ individuals on campus serves as a beacon of hope, challenging the prevailing norms and dismantling the barriers that often marginalize these communities.

Theoretical Framework

The concept of visibility in LGBTQ activism can be understood through the lens of *Queer Theory*, which posits that identity is not fixed but fluid, shaped by societal norms and cultural contexts. Judith Butler's theory of gender performativity suggests that gender is an act, and by increasing visibility, individuals can challenge and redefine these acts. The more LGBTQ individuals are visible, the more they can disrupt the traditional narratives surrounding gender and sexuality, paving the way for broader acceptance and understanding.

Challenges in Visibility

Despite the theoretical advantages of visibility, several challenges persist. Many LGBTQ students face the fear of backlash, discrimination, or ostracization, which can inhibit their willingness to be visible. The stigma surrounding LGBTQ identities often manifests in microaggressions and overt discrimination, which create a hostile environment.

Moreover, the intersectionality of identities means that visibility is not uniform. LGBTQ individuals of color, those with disabilities, and other marginalized groups within the community may experience compounded challenges, leading to their further invisibility.

Strategies for Increasing Visibility

Vex implemented several strategies to enhance LGBTQ visibility on campus:

- **Awareness Campaigns:** Vex spearheaded awareness campaigns that showcased LGBTQ stories and experiences. Utilizing social media platforms, posters, and events, these campaigns highlighted the diversity within the LGBTQ community, encouraging students to share their narratives.

- **LGBTQ Resource Center:** Establishing a dedicated LGBTQ Resource Center on campus provided a safe space for students to gather, seek support, and engage in dialogue. The center hosted workshops, discussions, and events that celebrated LGBTQ identities and fostered allyship.

- **Visibility Events:** Organizing events such as "Coming Out Day" and "Trans Awareness Week" created opportunities for students to express their identities openly. These events featured speakers, panel discussions, and artistic performances that celebrated LGBTQ culture and history.

- **Collaborations with Faculty:** Vex encouraged faculty members to incorporate LGBTQ topics into their curricula. By promoting LGBTQ literature, history, and theory, students could see their identities reflected in academic discourse, thus validating their experiences.

- **Visibility in Leadership:** Vex emphasized the importance of LGBTQ representation in student government and leadership positions. By ensuring that LGBTQ voices were included in decision-making processes, the community could influence policies that directly affected their lives.

Impact of Increased Visibility

The impact of these initiatives was profound. The campus environment began to shift as more students felt empowered to express their identities. Vex's leadership inspired others to take action, leading to the formation of new student organizations focused on LGBTQ issues.

Moreover, studies have shown that increased visibility positively correlates with mental health outcomes for LGBTQ individuals. According to a survey conducted by the *Human Rights Campaign*, LGBTQ youth who feel accepted and visible are 40% less likely to experience depression and anxiety.

Examples of Success

One notable success was the annual Kaevin Pride Week, which Vex organized. The event attracted hundreds of participants, including allies and community members, fostering a sense of unity and celebration. The visibility of LGBTQ individuals during this week not only empowered those within the community but also educated the broader campus about LGBTQ issues.

Additionally, Vex collaborated with local businesses to sponsor events, thereby extending the visibility of LGBTQ issues beyond the campus and into the larger community. This partnership not only amplified the message of inclusivity but also demonstrated the economic impact of supporting LGBTQ visibility.

Conclusion

Boosting LGBTQ visibility on campus was a cornerstone of Vex Aleron's activism. By employing strategic initiatives rooted in theory and community engagement, Vex transformed the campus into a more inclusive space. The journey was fraught with challenges, but the resulting visibility fostered understanding, acceptance, and a renewed commitment to equality. As Vex often reminded peers, visibility is not just about being seen; it is about being recognized, valued, and celebrated for one's authentic self.

Inspiring Other Youth Leaders

In the vibrant landscape of LGBTQ activism, the role of youth leaders is pivotal. Vex Aleron, through their tenacity and vision, not only carved a path for themselves but also illuminated the way for other young activists in Kaevin. This section explores how Vex inspired a new generation of leaders, emphasizing the importance of mentorship, visibility, and the cultivation of a supportive community.

The Importance of Mentorship

Mentorship serves as a cornerstone in the development of effective youth leaders. Vex recognized that their journey was not merely a personal quest for identity and equality, but a collective movement that required the involvement of many. By establishing mentorship programs within the Student Alliance for Equality, Vex created a structured environment where experienced activists could guide newcomers. This approach aligns with Bandura's Social Learning Theory, which posits that individuals learn from observing others.

$$B = f(P, E) \tag{7}$$

where B is behavior, P is personal factors, and E is environmental influences. Vex's mentorship initiative exemplified this theory, as young activists observed and emulated the strategies of seasoned leaders, thereby enhancing their own activism skills.

Visibility and Representation

Visibility is crucial in inspiring other youth leaders. Vex understood that representation matters; seeing someone who mirrors their own identity can empower young individuals to step into leadership roles. By actively participating in public forums, media interviews, and community events, Vex showcased the diversity within the LGBTQ community.

For instance, during the annual Kaevin Pride Parade, Vex invited youth from various backgrounds to share their stories on stage, ensuring that voices often marginalized were amplified. This act of representation not only inspired those who spoke but also resonated with countless others in the audience, fostering a sense of belonging and encouraging them to engage in activism.

Creating a Supportive Community

A supportive community is essential for nurturing leadership among youth. Vex emphasized the importance of building an inclusive environment where all individuals felt valued and empowered. This involved organizing workshops and retreats focused on personal development, leadership skills, and team-building exercises.

One notable example was the "Empowerment Retreat" held in Kaevin's local community center, where young activists participated in activities designed to enhance their confidence and collaborative skills. The retreat included sessions on public speaking, conflict resolution, and effective communication strategies. The feedback from participants was overwhelmingly positive, with many expressing that the experience had reignited their passion for activism and equipped them with the necessary tools to lead.

Encouraging Collaboration Among Youth Leaders

Vex also understood the power of collaboration among youth leaders. By fostering partnerships between different student organizations and community groups, Vex created a network of young activists who could share resources, ideas, and strategies. This collaborative spirit was evident in the "Youth Activism Summit," where diverse groups came together to discuss pressing issues facing the LGBTQ community in Kaevin.

The summit featured workshops led by youth leaders who had successfully implemented change in their own organizations. For example, a workshop on "Creating Safe Spaces in Schools" led by a group of high school students who had successfully advocated for inclusive policies in their district served as a powerful testament to the impact of youth-led initiatives.

Utilizing Technology for Inspiration

In the digital age, technology plays a crucial role in inspiring and mobilizing youth leaders. Vex harnessed the power of social media platforms to amplify their message and connect with other young activists. By sharing their journey, challenges, and successes online, Vex created a relatable narrative that resonated with many.

For instance, Vex launched a campaign on social media titled "#KaevinYouthVoices," encouraging young people to share their stories of activism. The campaign went viral, leading to an influx of new youth leaders who were eager to make their voices heard. This highlights the importance of digital platforms in fostering community and inspiring action.

Conclusion

Inspiring other youth leaders is not merely about imparting knowledge; it is about creating an environment where young individuals feel empowered to take action. Through mentorship, visibility, community support, collaboration, and the strategic use of technology, Vex Aleron not only shaped their own path but also ignited a spark in countless others. As these young leaders continue to rise, they carry forward the legacy of activism, ensuring that the fight for LGBTQ equality in Kaevin endures for generations to come.

Facing Backlash and Resistance

Dealing with Homophobic Attacks

Homophobic attacks are a pervasive issue faced by many within the LGBTQ community, particularly for activists like Vex Aleron, who challenge societal norms and advocate for equality. These attacks can manifest in various forms, including verbal harassment, physical violence, and systemic discrimination. Understanding the nature of these attacks and developing strategies to cope with and combat them is essential for both personal resilience and broader social change.

The Nature of Homophobic Attacks

Homophobic attacks are often rooted in deeply ingrained societal prejudices. According to [2], homophobia can be defined as an irrational fear or aversion to individuals who identify as LGBTQ. This fear often translates into hostility and aggression, creating an environment where LGBTQ individuals feel unsafe. The **Social Identity Theory** posits that individuals derive part of their identity from the groups to which they belong, leading to in-group favoritism and out-group discrimination [2]. Consequently, when an individual identifies as LGBTQ, they may become a target for those who perceive their identity as a threat to traditional social norms.

The Impact of Homophobic Attacks

The consequences of homophobic attacks extend beyond immediate physical harm. Victims often experience long-term psychological effects, including anxiety, depression, and post-traumatic stress disorder (PTSD) [1]. For example, Vex faced verbal harassment during a school assembly, which not only affected their self-esteem but also instilled a sense of fear that permeated their daily life. The psychological toll of such experiences can hinder one's ability to engage in activism and community-building efforts.

Strategies for Coping and Resilience

1. **Building Support Networks:** One of the most effective ways to cope with homophobic attacks is to establish a robust support network. Friends, family, and community organizations can provide emotional support and practical assistance. Vex found solace in the Student Alliance for Equality, where they connected with peers who shared similar experiences and could offer understanding and encouragement.

2. **Education and Awareness:** Raising awareness about the realities of homophobic attacks can help dismantle stereotypes and reduce prejudice. Activists like Vex have utilized workshops and educational campaigns to inform their peers about the impact of homophobia. By sharing personal stories and statistics, they foster empathy and understanding, creating a safer environment for all.

3. **Reporting and Legal Action:** It is crucial to document and report homophobic attacks. Many jurisdictions have laws protecting individuals from

hate crimes, and reporting these incidents can lead to legal action against perpetrators. Vex encouraged their peers to report attacks to school authorities, which led to increased vigilance and awareness within the institution.

Case Studies and Examples

Several notable incidents highlight the challenges faced by LGBTQ activists in dealing with homophobic attacks. For instance, the 2016 Pulse nightclub shooting in Orlando, Florida, serves as a grim reminder of the violence that can erupt against the LGBTQ community. This tragedy galvanized activists worldwide, leading to increased calls for gun control and anti-discrimination legislation. Vex often referenced this incident in their speeches, emphasizing the need for solidarity and action to prevent such violence.

In contrast, smaller-scale incidents, such as Vex's experience with verbal harassment during a local pride event, illustrate the everyday challenges faced by LGBTQ individuals. Vex responded to the harassment by organizing a workshop on bystander intervention, empowering others to stand up against homophobia in real-time.

Conclusion

Dealing with homophobic attacks is a multifaceted challenge that requires resilience, community support, and proactive measures. By understanding the nature of these attacks, their impact, and effective coping strategies, individuals like Vex Aleron can continue to advocate for LGBTQ rights while fostering a culture of acceptance and understanding. The fight against homophobia is ongoing, but with collective effort and determination, progress can be made toward a more inclusive society.

Battling Misinformation and Hate Speech

In the landscape of LGBTQ activism, misinformation and hate speech represent formidable barriers to progress. These challenges not only undermine the credibility of the movement but also perpetuate harmful stereotypes and foster an environment of intolerance. This section explores the theoretical underpinnings of misinformation and hate speech, the problems they pose to LGBTQ advocacy, and notable examples of activism aimed at combating these issues.

Theoretical Framework

Misinformation can be understood through the lens of the *knowledge deficit model*, which posits that individuals hold inaccurate beliefs due to a lack of information. This model suggests that simply providing accurate information can resolve misunderstandings. However, research indicates that misinformation often persists even in the face of factual correction, a phenomenon known as the *backfire effect* [1]. This effect demonstrates that when individuals are confronted with information that contradicts their beliefs, they may cling more tightly to their misconceptions.

Hate speech, on the other hand, is defined by its intent to incite violence or prejudicial action against a particular group. The *social identity theory* posits that individuals derive a sense of self from their group memberships, leading to in-group favoritism and out-group discrimination [2]. Hate speech can exacerbate this division, reinforcing negative stereotypes and creating a hostile environment for marginalized communities.

Problems Posed by Misinformation and Hate Speech

The prevalence of misinformation and hate speech can have dire consequences for LGBTQ individuals and the broader movement for equality. Firstly, misinformation can lead to public misunderstanding of LGBTQ issues, which can manifest in discriminatory policies and practices. For instance, false narratives regarding the mental health of LGBTQ individuals have been used to justify discriminatory legislation, such as conversion therapy bans being challenged on the grounds of "protecting" individuals from purported mental health risks [3].

Secondly, hate speech can incite violence against LGBTQ individuals. The FBI reported that hate crimes based on sexual orientation and gender identity have been on the rise, contributing to a climate of fear and insecurity within the community [4]. The normalization of hate speech in public discourse can embolden individuals to act on these harmful beliefs, leading to real-world violence and discrimination.

Examples of Activism Against Misinformation and Hate Speech

Activists have employed various strategies to combat misinformation and hate speech within their communities. One notable example is the *"It Gets Better"* campaign, which was launched in response to a spate of suicides among LGBTQ youth. This initiative utilized social media platforms to share positive narratives and counteract the harmful messages that often dominate discussions about

LGBTQ lives. By amplifying stories of resilience and success, the campaign aimed to provide hope and challenge negative stereotypes.

Another effective approach has been the development of educational programs aimed at dispelling myths about LGBTQ individuals. Organizations such as GLAAD have created resources that provide factual information about LGBTQ identities, relationships, and rights. These resources are designed to be easily accessible and are often shared through social media channels to reach a broad audience.

Furthermore, legal frameworks are being leveraged to address hate speech. For example, the *Equality Act* in the United States aims to expand protections against discrimination based on sexual orientation and gender identity, thereby addressing the systemic issues that allow hate speech to proliferate. Activists are working to ensure that such legislation is passed and enforced, recognizing that legal protections are essential in the fight against hate.

Conclusion

Battling misinformation and hate speech is an ongoing struggle within the LGBTQ rights movement. By employing a combination of education, community engagement, and legal advocacy, activists like Vex Aleron are working tirelessly to create a safer and more inclusive environment for all. The fight against these insidious forces requires resilience and creativity, as the stakes are high and the consequences of inaction can be devastating. As the movement continues to evolve, addressing misinformation and hate speech will remain a critical component of the quest for equality.

Bibliography

[1] Lewandowsky, S., Ecker, U. K. H., & Cook, J. (2012). Beyond Misinformation: Understanding and Coping with the "Post-Truth" Era. *Journal of Applied Research in Memory and Cognition*, 1(2), 120-128.

[2] Tajfel, H., & Turner, J. C. (1979). An Integrative Theory of Intergroup Conflict. In W. G. Austin & S. Worchel (Eds.), *The Social Psychology of Intergroup Relations* (pp. 33-47). Monterey, CA: Brooks/Cole.

[3] American Psychological Association. (2015). Report of the American Psychological Association Task Force on Appropriate Therapeutic Responses to Sexual Orientation. Retrieved from https://www.apa.org/pi/lgbt/resources/therapeutic-response.pdf

[4] Federal Bureau of Investigation. (2020). Hate Crime Statistics, 2019. Retrieved from https://ucr.fbi.gov/hate-crime/2020

Building Resilience in the Face of Adversity

Building resilience is a crucial aspect of navigating the challenges faced by LGBTQ activists, particularly in a society that often presents significant opposition to their rights and identities. Resilience can be defined as the ability to recover from setbacks, adapt to change, and keep going in the face of adversity. In the context of LGBTQ activism, resilience is not just a personal trait but a collective necessity, enabling individuals and communities to withstand the pressures of discrimination, hostility, and societal rejection.

Theoretical frameworks surrounding resilience often draw from psychology and social science. One prominent theory is the **Ecological Model of Resilience**, which posits that resilience is influenced by the interplay of individual, relational, community, and societal factors. This model highlights that while personal characteristics such as optimism and self-efficacy play a role, the support systems surrounding an individual—such as family, friends, and community organizations—are equally critical in fostering resilience.

$$R = f(I, S, C, E) \tag{8}$$

Where: - R = Resilience - I = Individual characteristics (e.g., self-esteem, coping strategies) - S = Social support (e.g., friends, family, community) - C = Community resources (e.g., LGBTQ organizations, safe spaces) - E = Environmental factors (e.g., societal attitudes, legal protections)

Individual Characteristics

For many LGBTQ activists, resilience begins with the cultivation of personal strength. This includes developing a strong sense of identity and self-acceptance. Research indicates that individuals who embrace their identities are better equipped to handle adversity. For instance, a study by [1] found that internalized homophobia can significantly undermine resilience, leading to mental health challenges. Conversely, activists who engage in self-affirmation practices—such as positive self-talk and community involvement—often report higher levels of resilience.

Social Support Networks

The role of social support cannot be overstated. Activists often find strength in their connections with others who share similar experiences. This can manifest in various forms, from informal friendships to formal support groups. For example, organizations like *The Trevor Project* provide critical emotional support and resources for LGBTQ youth facing adversity. Research shows that having a reliable support network can buffer against the negative effects of discrimination and stress, enhancing an individual's ability to cope with challenges [?].

Community Resources

Community organizations play a vital role in fostering resilience among LGBTQ activists. By providing safe spaces, resources, and advocacy, these organizations help individuals navigate the complexities of activism. For instance, the establishment of LGBTQ centers in various cities has proven effective in creating environments where individuals can connect, share experiences, and strategize for change. The availability of mental health services tailored to LGBTQ individuals also contributes to building resilience, as these services address the unique challenges faced by this community [?].

Environmental Factors

Environmental factors, including societal attitudes and legal protections, significantly impact resilience. Activists in regions with supportive laws and progressive social attitudes often report higher resilience levels compared to those in more hostile environments. For example, in countries where same-sex marriage is legal and anti-discrimination laws are enforced, LGBTQ activists may experience less psychological stress and greater community support, enabling them to pursue their goals more effectively [?].

Examples of Resilience in Action

One poignant example of resilience in the face of adversity can be seen in the story of Vex Aleron, who faced significant backlash after organizing a protest for LGBTQ rights in Kaevin. Despite receiving threats and facing public ridicule, Aleron utilized coping strategies learned from previous experiences and leaned on their support network of friends and fellow activists. By reframing the narrative around their activism and focusing on the positive impact of their work, Aleron not only managed to overcome personal challenges but also inspired others in the community to stand firm against adversity.

Additionally, the response to the backlash faced by the Kaevin Pride Parade highlights collective resilience. Activists banded together, organizing workshops and community forums to address the homophobia and transphobia that emerged in response to the parade. This collective action not only strengthened the community's resolve but also fostered a sense of unity and purpose among individuals who may have felt isolated in their struggles.

Conclusion

Building resilience in the face of adversity is a multifaceted process that involves individual determination, social support, community resources, and a favorable environment. For LGBTQ activists, resilience is essential not only for personal well-being but also for the success of the broader movement for equality. By understanding and harnessing the factors that contribute to resilience, activists can better navigate the challenges they face and continue to advocate for a more inclusive and equitable society.

Confronting Prejudice within the LGBTQ Community

Within the LGBTQ community, the fight for equality does not solely exist against external societal norms; it often extends into the very fabric of the community itself. This internal prejudice can manifest in various forms, including racism, transphobia, and classism, creating a complex web of challenges that activists like Vex Aleron must navigate.

Understanding Internalized Prejudice

Internalized prejudice occurs when individuals adopt the negative stereotypes and biases that society holds against their own group. This phenomenon can be particularly pronounced in LGBTQ individuals who may struggle with their identities due to societal stigma. According to [?], internalized homophobia can lead to self-hatred, depression, and a reluctance to engage with the broader LGBTQ community.

Vex recognized that confronting this internalized prejudice was crucial for fostering a more inclusive environment. By organizing workshops and support groups, Vex aimed to create safe spaces where individuals could express their struggles and challenges without fear of judgment. This initiative provided a platform for members to share their experiences, highlighting the importance of mutual support in overcoming internalized biases.

Racism and Intersectionality

One of the most pressing issues within the LGBTQ community is the intersection of race and sexual orientation. Studies, such as those conducted by [?], have shown that LGBTQ people of color often face compounded discrimination that can alienate them from both the broader LGBTQ community and their racial communities. This marginalization can lead to feelings of isolation and a lack of representation in LGBTQ spaces.

Vex's activism included addressing these intersectional issues head-on. By collaborating with organizations focused on racial justice, Vex worked to ensure that the voices of LGBTQ people of color were amplified. Events like the Kaevin Pride Parade became platforms for showcasing diverse identities, allowing individuals to celebrate their multifaceted experiences rather than conforming to a singular narrative.

Transphobia in the LGBTQ Community

Transphobia is another critical issue that Vex sought to confront within the LGBTQ community. Despite being part of the same community, transgender individuals often face discrimination from their peers, leading to a culture of exclusion. According to [?], trans individuals are disproportionately affected by violence and discrimination, not only from society at large but also from within LGBTQ spaces.

Vex initiated educational campaigns aimed at informing community members about transgender issues, emphasizing the importance of allyship. Workshops were held to discuss appropriate language, the significance of pronouns, and the unique challenges faced by transgender individuals. By fostering a culture of understanding and respect, Vex hoped to dismantle the transphobia that persisted within the LGBTQ community.

Classism and Economic Disparities

Classism is another form of prejudice that can affect LGBTQ individuals, particularly in terms of access to resources and opportunities. Economic disparities can create barriers that prevent marginalized individuals from participating fully in LGBTQ activism. Vex recognized that many activists came from privileged backgrounds, which could inadvertently alienate those who did not share the same socioeconomic status.

To address these disparities, Vex advocated for inclusive policies that considered the needs of lower-income LGBTQ individuals. This included organizing fundraising events to support local LGBTQ organizations that provided resources such as housing assistance, healthcare, and job training for those in need. By promoting economic equity within the community, Vex aimed to create a more inclusive environment where all voices could be heard.

Creating a Culture of Inclusivity

Ultimately, confronting prejudice within the LGBTQ community requires a concerted effort to foster a culture of inclusivity. Vex emphasized the importance of allyship and solidarity among community members. By encouraging open dialogues about race, gender, and class, Vex aimed to cultivate an environment where individuals could learn from one another and challenge their biases.

As part of this initiative, Vex launched a series of community forums where members could engage in discussions about their experiences with prejudice. These forums served as a space for reflection and growth, allowing individuals to confront their biases and work towards collective healing.

In conclusion, confronting prejudice within the LGBTQ community is an ongoing challenge that requires vigilance and commitment. Activists like Vex Aleron play a crucial role in addressing these issues, fostering a more inclusive environment that recognizes and celebrates diversity. Through education, collaboration, and open dialogue, the LGBTQ community can work towards dismantling the prejudices that hinder its progress, ultimately creating a more equitable society for all.

Rising Above Negativity

In the journey of activism, particularly within the LGBTQ community, rising above negativity is not just a personal challenge; it is a collective necessity. Vex Aleron, much like many young activists, faced an onslaught of negativity that ranged from personal attacks to systemic discrimination. Understanding the psychological and sociological implications of this negativity is essential for fostering resilience among activists.

The Psychological Impact of Negativity

The impact of negativity on mental health can be profound. Studies indicate that exposure to homophobic remarks and discrimination can lead to increased levels of anxiety and depression among LGBTQ individuals. According to the *American Psychological Association*, individuals who experience discrimination are at a higher risk of developing mental health issues, which can hinder their ability to engage in activism effectively.

To combat these effects, Vex adopted several strategies grounded in psychological resilience theory. This theory posits that resilience can be cultivated through positive relationships, self-awareness, and adaptive coping mechanisms. Vex sought support from peers and mentors who understood the unique challenges faced by LGBTQ activists, creating a network of solidarity that served as a buffer against negativity.

Cognitive Reframing

One of the key strategies Vex employed was cognitive reframing, a technique rooted in cognitive-behavioral therapy. By changing the narrative around negative experiences, Vex was able to transform feelings of helplessness into a sense of agency. For instance, when faced with homophobic slurs during protests, Vex reframed these attacks as opportunities to educate the public about LGBTQ issues. This shift not only mitigated the emotional toll of the negativity but also galvanized support from allies who witnessed Vex's unwavering commitment to the cause.

$$\text{Resilience} = \frac{\text{Support} + \text{Positive Reframing}}{\text{Negativity}} \qquad (9)$$

This equation illustrates that resilience can be viewed as a function of the support one receives and the ability to reframe negative experiences, divided by the amount of negativity encountered. By increasing the numerator through community support and reframing, Vex effectively diminished the influence of negativity.

Building a Positive Narrative

In the face of adversity, Vex recognized the importance of creating a positive narrative around LGBTQ activism. This involved highlighting success stories, showcasing the progress made in the fight for equality, and amplifying the voices of marginalized individuals within the community. By focusing on positive outcomes, Vex was able to inspire others to join the movement, reinforcing the idea that collective action could lead to meaningful change.

For example, during the organization of the first Kaevin Pride Parade, Vex faced significant opposition from conservative groups. Instead of succumbing to despair, Vex used social media platforms to share stories of LGBTQ individuals who had benefited from previous activism. This approach not only countered the negativity but also rallied support from allies who were moved by the personal narratives of resilience and courage.

Engaging with Critics Constructively

Another critical aspect of rising above negativity involved engaging with critics constructively. Vex understood that not all opposition stemmed from hatred; some arose from misunderstanding. By adopting an approach rooted in empathy and education, Vex sought to engage in dialogue with those who held opposing views. This strategy not only diffused tension but also opened avenues for potential allies.

For instance, when faced with backlash from local religious institutions, Vex organized community forums where LGBTQ individuals could share their experiences and address misconceptions. This initiative fostered a space for dialogue, allowing individuals to confront their biases and engage in meaningful conversations about LGBTQ rights.

The Role of Community Support

Ultimately, rising above negativity hinges on the strength of community support. Vex's journey exemplified the power of collective resilience. By fostering an inclusive environment where individuals felt safe to express themselves, Vex helped cultivate a culture of acceptance and understanding. This community not only provided emotional support but also served as a powerful counter-narrative to the negativity faced by LGBTQ activists.

In conclusion, rising above negativity is an ongoing process that requires intentional effort, emotional intelligence, and a commitment to fostering positive relationships. Vex Aleron's journey illustrates that while negativity can be pervasive, it does not have to define the narrative of LGBTQ activism. By employing strategies such as cognitive reframing, building positive narratives, engaging with critics, and relying on community support, activists can not only withstand the challenges they face but also emerge stronger and more united in their pursuit of equality.

Chapter 2

Pushing Boundaries

Organizing the First Kaevin Pride Parade

In the heart of Kaevin, a city steeped in tradition and often resistant to change, the idea of a Pride Parade was met with a mixture of excitement and trepidation. The journey to organizing the first Kaevin Pride Parade was not merely about celebration; it was a bold statement of identity, resilience, and a demand for visibility in a society that had long marginalized LGBTQ voices.

The Vision

The initial vision for the parade was born out of a desire to create a safe space for LGBTQ individuals to express their identities openly and proudly. This vision was rooted in the theory of *social identity*, which posits that individuals derive part of their self-concept from their perceived membership in social groups. The parade would serve as a public affirmation of LGBTQ identity, fostering community solidarity and challenging societal norms.

Gathering Support

To transform this vision into reality, Vex Aleron, along with fellow activists from the Student Alliance for Equality, began by gathering support from various stakeholders. This included local businesses, LGBTQ organizations, and allies within the community. The initial meetings were crucial, as they not only helped to build a coalition but also to identify potential challenges.

A significant challenge was the lack of awareness and understanding of LGBTQ issues among the general population. To address this, the team organized informational sessions to educate the community about the importance of the parade. These sessions highlighted the historical significance of Pride events worldwide, linking them to the broader struggle for human rights.

Legal Hurdles

One of the most pressing issues was navigating the legal framework required to hold a public event in Kaevin. The team faced bureaucratic hurdles that included obtaining permits and complying with local regulations. This process was fraught with obstacles, as city officials were skeptical about the parade's potential impact on public order.

Vex and the team utilized the theory of *collective efficacy*, which refers to the shared belief in the group's ability to achieve goals. They organized rallies and petitions, demonstrating community support for the parade. The overwhelming response from the public showcased the demand for change, leading to a gradual shift in the city's stance.

Engaging the Community

With legal permissions finally secured, the next step was to engage the community actively. Vex emphasized the importance of inclusivity, ensuring that the parade represented the diverse spectrum of the LGBTQ community. This involved reaching out to various groups, including transgender individuals, people of color, and those with disabilities, ensuring their voices were heard in the planning process.

The organizing committee created a series of workshops to involve community members in the design of floats, banners, and performances. This participatory approach not only fostered a sense of ownership among participants but also highlighted the intersectionality within the LGBTQ community, addressing the unique challenges faced by different groups.

Promoting the Event

As the date of the parade approached, the team launched an extensive promotional campaign. Utilizing social media platforms, local radio stations, and community bulletin boards, they spread the word about the event. They crafted messages that emphasized themes of love, acceptance, and pride, aiming to counteract the negative narratives often associated with LGBTQ visibility.

A notable example of their promotional efforts was the creation of a video campaign featuring testimonials from community members discussing what Pride meant to them. This campaign not only humanized the cause but also encouraged allies to participate, thereby broadening the parade's reach.

The Day of the Parade

On the day of the first Kaevin Pride Parade, the atmosphere was electric. Participants adorned in vibrant colors filled the streets, embodying the spirit of joy and defiance. The parade commenced with a rally at the city square, where Vex delivered an impassioned speech that resonated with the crowd.

The speech touched upon the struggles faced by the LGBTQ community in Kaevin and the significance of the parade as a step towards equality. Vex articulated the challenges of being queer in a traditional society, emphasizing the importance of visibility and representation.

Challenges Faced During the Parade

Despite the jubilant atmosphere, the parade was not without its challenges. A small group of counter-protesters attempted to disrupt the event, wielding signs filled with hate speech. However, the organizing team had anticipated such a reaction and had coordinated with local law enforcement to ensure the safety of participants.

This incident underscored the ongoing battle against homophobia and transphobia in Kaevin. It also highlighted the need for continued activism and dialogue to foster understanding and acceptance.

Reflections and Impact

In the aftermath of the parade, Vex and the organizing committee reflected on the event's impact. The parade not only brought visibility to the LGBTQ community but also sparked conversations across Kaevin about acceptance and equality.

The success of the first Kaevin Pride Parade laid the groundwork for future events and initiatives, reinforcing the idea that activism is a continuous journey. It also served as a reminder that while challenges may arise, the power of community and collective action can lead to meaningful change.

Conclusion

Organizing the first Kaevin Pride Parade was a transformative experience for Vex Aleron and the community. It was a testament to the power of resilience, the importance of visibility, and the ongoing fight for LGBTQ rights. The parade not only celebrated diversity but also paved the way for future generations to embrace their identities without fear or shame. In the words of Vex, "Pride is not just a celebration; it's a declaration of our existence and our right to love freely."

Confronting Homophobia and Transphobia

In the vibrant tapestry of LGBTQ activism, confronting homophobia and transphobia is an essential thread. These forms of discrimination not only harm individuals but also undermine the very fabric of society by perpetuating inequality and injustice. Vex Aleron, as a young activist in Kaevin, recognized that tackling these issues head-on was crucial for fostering a more inclusive community.

Understanding Homophobia and Transphobia

Homophobia refers to the fear, hatred, or prejudice against individuals who identify as LGBTQ, while transphobia specifically targets transgender and non-binary individuals. These attitudes can manifest in various forms, from overt violence and discrimination to subtle microaggressions. According to the *American Psychological Association*, homophobia and transphobia can lead to significant mental health issues, including anxiety, depression, and suicidal ideation among affected individuals.

Theoretical Frameworks

To effectively confront these prejudices, it is essential to understand the underlying theories that inform them. One prominent theory is **Social Identity Theory** (Tajfel & Turner, 1979), which posits that individuals derive a sense of self from their group memberships. This can lead to in-group favoritism and out-group discrimination. In the context of LGBTQ issues, those who identify as heterosexual may feel threatened by the visibility and rights of LGBTQ individuals, leading to defensive reactions characterized by homophobia and transphobia.

Additionally, the **Intersectionality Framework** (Crenshaw, 1989) emphasizes that individuals experience overlapping identities that can compound discrimination. For instance, a queer person of color may face unique challenges that differ from those encountered by white LGBTQ individuals. This understanding is vital for developing comprehensive strategies to combat prejudice.

Identifying Problems

Homophobia and transphobia present numerous challenges within society, including:

- **Violence and Harassment:** LGBTQ individuals often face physical violence, harassment, and even murder due to their sexual orientation or gender identity. According to the *Human Rights Campaign*, hate crimes against LGBTQ individuals have seen a troubling increase in recent years.

- **Discrimination in Employment and Housing:** Many LGBTQ individuals experience discrimination in the workplace, leading to economic instability and job insecurity. Similarly, housing discrimination can leave individuals without safe and stable living conditions.

- **Mental Health Issues:** The stress of living in a homophobic or transphobic environment can lead to severe mental health challenges. Studies have shown that LGBTQ individuals are at a higher risk for depression and anxiety due to societal rejection.

Examples of Confrontation

Vex Aleron's activism in Kaevin included a multifaceted approach to confronting homophobia and transphobia:

1. **Educational Workshops:** Aleron organized workshops in schools and community centers aimed at educating individuals about LGBTQ issues. These sessions included discussions about the harmful effects of homophobia and transphobia, emphasizing empathy and understanding. By fostering dialogue, Aleron sought to dismantle stereotypes and promote acceptance.

2. **Visibility Campaigns:** Understanding the power of representation, Aleron launched visibility campaigns that showcased LGBTQ individuals' stories, achievements, and contributions to society. These campaigns aimed to humanize LGBTQ experiences and challenge the negative narratives perpetuated by homophobia and transphobia.

3. **Collaborating with Law Enforcement:** Aleron worked with local law enforcement agencies to address hate crimes and improve responses to incidents of violence against LGBTQ individuals. This collaboration included training officers on LGBTQ issues and creating safe reporting mechanisms for victims.

The Role of Allies

Allies play a crucial role in confronting homophobia and transphobia. Aleron emphasized the importance of allyship in their activism, encouraging individuals outside the LGBTQ community to stand in solidarity. Allies can help amplify

LGBTQ voices, challenge discriminatory remarks, and advocate for inclusive policies.

Conclusion

Confronting homophobia and transphobia is a continuous journey that requires collective effort and commitment. Through education, visibility, and allyship, activists like Vex Aleron are paving the way for a more inclusive society in Kaevin. By addressing these issues head-on, they not only challenge the status quo but also inspire others to join the fight for equality and acceptance.

$$\text{Empathy} + \text{Education} + \text{Advocacy} = \text{Progress} \tag{10}$$

Engaging with Religious Institutions

Engaging with religious institutions is a critical aspect of LGBTQ activism, particularly in societies like Kaevin, where traditional beliefs often intersect with modern values. Activists like Vex Aleron recognized that to foster genuine dialogue and promote LGBTQ rights, it was essential to address the concerns and beliefs of religious groups. This section explores the challenges faced, strategies employed, and the impact of these engagements on the broader movement for equality.

Understanding Religious Perspectives

Religious institutions often hold significant sway over societal norms and values. In Kaevin, many religious groups maintain traditional views on sexuality and gender identity, which can lead to resistance against LGBTQ rights. Understanding these perspectives is crucial for activists. For instance, many religious doctrines emphasize the sanctity of heterosexual relationships and may view LGBTQ identities as contrary to their beliefs. Engaging with these institutions requires a nuanced approach that respects their beliefs while advocating for inclusivity.

Identifying Common Ground

One effective strategy employed by Vex was to identify common ground with religious leaders. Many religious teachings promote love, compassion, and acceptance, values that resonate with LGBTQ activism. By framing discussions around these shared values, activists can create a more conducive environment for dialogue. For example, Vex organized interfaith panels where religious leaders and

LGBTQ activists could share their experiences and perspectives, fostering understanding and empathy.

Addressing Misconceptions

A significant barrier to acceptance is the misconceptions surrounding LGBTQ identities within religious communities. Many religious individuals may believe that being LGBTQ is a choice or a sin. Activists like Vex worked to dispel these myths by providing educational resources and personal testimonies. For instance, hosting workshops that include LGBTQ individuals who share their stories can humanize the issues and challenge preconceived notions.

Collaborative Initiatives

Vex also initiated collaborative projects with progressive religious groups that support LGBTQ rights. These initiatives included joint community service events, where LGBTQ activists and religious groups worked together to address social issues such as homelessness, poverty, and mental health. This collaboration not only strengthened community ties but also demonstrated that faith and acceptance can coexist.

Navigating Conflicts

Despite the potential for collaboration, conflicts often arise when engaging with religious institutions. For example, during the planning of the first Kaevin Pride Parade, Vex faced pushback from conservative religious groups who threatened to protest the event. Instead of retreating, Vex reached out to these groups, inviting them to a dialogue about the importance of the parade and its message of love and acceptance. This proactive approach helped to mitigate tensions and foster a more inclusive atmosphere for the event.

Long-Term Impact

The efforts to engage with religious institutions have had a lasting impact on the LGBTQ rights movement in Kaevin. By fostering dialogue and understanding, Vex and other activists have gradually shifted perceptions within some religious communities. For instance, several churches have begun to adopt LGBTQ-inclusive policies, offering support and affirmation to LGBTQ congregants. This shift not only benefits individuals but also contributes to a broader cultural change towards acceptance and equality.

Conclusion

Engaging with religious institutions is a complex but necessary endeavor in the fight for LGBTQ rights. By understanding perspectives, identifying common ground, addressing misconceptions, and navigating conflicts, activists like Vex Aleron have been able to create meaningful dialogue and foster change. This engagement not only strengthens the LGBTQ movement but also promotes a more inclusive society, where love and acceptance can thrive across all communities.

$$\text{Engagement Success} = \frac{\text{Common Ground} \times \text{Understanding}}{\text{Misconceptions} + \text{Conflicts}} \quad (11)$$

In this equation, the success of engagement with religious institutions is influenced by the ability to find common ground and mutual understanding, while being challenged by existing misconceptions and conflicts. The more effectively activists can address these issues, the greater the potential for fostering acceptance and equality within these influential institutions.

Navigating Legal Challenges

Navigating the legal landscape surrounding LGBTQ rights is akin to traversing a labyrinth filled with obstacles, each turn presenting its own unique challenges. For Vex Aleron, the journey began with the realization that the fight for equality was not just a social movement but also a legal battleground where laws could either empower or impede progress.

Understanding the Legal Framework

The first step in addressing legal challenges was to thoroughly understand the existing laws and regulations governing LGBTQ rights in Kaevin. This involved delving into local, state, and national statutes, as well as international human rights treaties that advocate for equality. Vex and the Student Alliance for Equality often found themselves poring over legal texts, deciphering complex language to identify loopholes and opportunities for advocacy.

$$\text{Legal Awareness} = \text{Research} + \text{Education} + \text{Community Engagement} \quad (12)$$

The equation above illustrates that legal awareness is not merely about individual research; it requires collective education and engagement with the community to foster a well-informed activist base.

Identifying Key Legal Issues

As Vex and their peers began to organize events such as the first Kaevin Pride Parade, they quickly identified several critical legal issues that needed to be addressed:

- **Anti-Discrimination Laws:** The absence of comprehensive anti-discrimination laws in employment, housing, and public accommodations left LGBTQ individuals vulnerable to bias and exclusion.

- **Marriage Equality:** The legal recognition of same-sex marriages was still a contentious issue, with many advocating for the right to marry being met with staunch opposition.

- **Transgender Rights:** Legal recognition of gender identity, including access to appropriate healthcare and documentation changes, was fraught with bureaucratic hurdles.

These issues not only affected individuals but also posed significant barriers to the broader movement for equality.

Strategizing Legal Action

To combat these challenges, Vex understood the importance of strategic legal action. This involved:

- **Collaborating with Legal Experts:** Partnering with lawyers and legal organizations that specialize in LGBTQ rights provided invaluable insights and resources. This collaboration resulted in well-drafted petitions and legal arguments that could withstand scrutiny.

- **Engaging in Litigation:** Vex and their allies initiated lawsuits against discriminatory practices, setting precedents that could benefit others in similar situations. One notable case involved challenging a local business's refusal to serve LGBTQ customers, which garnered significant media attention and public support.

- **Advocating for Legislative Change:** By mobilizing community support, they lobbied local lawmakers to introduce bills aimed at enhancing LGBTQ protections. This grassroots effort culminated in a landmark bill that expanded anti-discrimination protections to include sexual orientation and gender identity.

Facing Legal Pushback

However, the path was not without its hurdles. Vex and the Student Alliance faced significant pushback from conservative groups and individuals who opposed the changes. Legal challenges came in the form of:

- **Restraining Orders:** Opponents sought restraining orders to prevent Pride events from taking place, arguing that they disrupted public order. Vex's team had to respond swiftly, demonstrating through legal channels that these events were protected under freedom of expression.
- **Defamation Lawsuits:** Some activists faced defamation lawsuits from businesses and individuals who felt threatened by the movement. This tactic aimed to silence dissent and instill fear in those advocating for change.

In response, Vex emphasized the importance of resilience and unity within the community.

Building a Support Network

To combat these challenges effectively, Vex recognized the necessity of building a robust support network. This included:

- **Legal Aid Clinics:** Establishing clinics that provided free legal advice to LGBTQ individuals facing discrimination or harassment ensured that no one had to navigate these challenges alone.
- **Public Awareness Campaigns:** By raising awareness of the legal issues at stake, Vex and their team educated the broader public, garnering support that translated into political pressure on lawmakers.
- **Coalition Building:** Collaborating with other marginalized groups amplified their voice, creating a united front against oppressive legal structures. This intersectional approach proved essential in navigating the complexities of legal advocacy.

Conclusion

In conclusion, navigating the legal challenges facing LGBTQ activists in Kaevin was a multifaceted endeavor that required a deep understanding of the law, strategic action, and community solidarity. Vex Aleron's journey exemplified the intricate dance between activism and legal advocacy, demonstrating that while the path to equality is fraught with obstacles, it is also rich with opportunities for growth, solidarity, and change. As Vex often remarked, "In the face of adversity, our strength lies in our unity and our unwavering commitment to justice."

$$\text{Activism Success} = \text{Legal Strategy} + \text{Community Support} + \text{Resilience} \qquad (13)$$

This equation encapsulates the essence of Vex's approach to overcoming legal challenges—an enduring testament to the power of collective action in the pursuit of equality.

Expanding the LGBTQ Rights Movement

In the pursuit of equality, the LGBTQ rights movement has continuously evolved, adapting to the changing sociopolitical landscape. This evolution is not merely a reaction to external pressures but a proactive engagement with the complexities of identity, culture, and rights. Vex Aleron, through their tireless activism, has played a pivotal role in expanding the LGBTQ rights movement in Kaevin and beyond, demonstrating that activism is a multifaceted endeavor that requires both innovation and solidarity.

Theoretical Framework

To understand the expansion of the LGBTQ rights movement, we can apply several theoretical frameworks, including intersectionality, social movement theory, and queer theory.

Intersectionality posits that individuals experience overlapping social identities, which can lead to unique experiences of oppression and privilege. This framework is essential for recognizing that the LGBTQ community is not monolithic; it encompasses diverse identities, including race, class, gender, and ability. For instance, the experiences of a Black transgender woman differ significantly from those of a white gay man. By acknowledging these differences, activists like Vex can address the specific needs of various subgroups within the LGBTQ community.

Social Movement Theory offers insights into how collective action can lead to social change. According to this theory, movements arise when there is a perceived injustice, a mobilizing structure, and a political opportunity. Vex's efforts to organize the first Kaevin Pride Parade exemplify this theory. The perceived injustice of systemic discrimination against LGBTQ individuals galvanized the community, while Vex's leadership provided the mobilizing structure necessary for action. The political opportunity arose from a growing public discourse on LGBTQ rights, which Vex and their allies seized to advocate for change.

Queer Theory challenges normative assumptions about gender and sexuality, advocating for a more fluid understanding of identity. This theoretical lens is crucial in expanding the LGBTQ rights movement to include diverse sexual orientations and gender identities. Vex's activism has emphasized the importance of recognizing and validating non-binary and gender-nonconforming identities, thereby broadening the movement's scope.

Challenges Faced

Despite significant progress, the expansion of the LGBTQ rights movement faces several challenges:

Internal Divisions within the LGBTQ community can hinder collective action. Different groups may prioritize distinct issues, leading to fragmentation. For example, the focus on marriage equality has sometimes overshadowed the urgent needs of transgender individuals, particularly regarding healthcare access and legal recognition. Vex has worked to bridge these divides by fostering dialogue and collaboration among various factions of the community.

External Resistance from conservative and religious groups poses another significant challenge. These groups often mobilize against LGBTQ rights, framing their arguments within traditional values and beliefs. For instance, the backlash against the Kaevin Pride Parade included organized protests by religious organizations that sought to undermine the event's legitimacy. Vex and their allies countered this resistance by engaging in respectful dialogue and emphasizing the importance of inclusivity and acceptance.

Legal and Political Barriers also impede progress. In many regions, discriminatory laws and policies persist, creating obstacles for LGBTQ individuals. For example, attempts to pass comprehensive anti-discrimination legislation in Kaevin have faced significant opposition. Vex has championed grassroots campaigns to educate the public and lobby lawmakers, demonstrating that sustained advocacy is essential for overcoming these barriers.

Successful Strategies for Expansion

To effectively expand the LGBTQ rights movement, Vex has implemented several successful strategies:

Grassroots Mobilization has been a cornerstone of Vex's approach. By organizing community events, workshops, and educational campaigns, they have empowered individuals to take action and advocate for their rights. This grassroots engagement fosters a sense of ownership within the community, encouraging collective responsibility for advancing LGBTQ rights.

Coalition Building with other marginalized groups has also been instrumental. Vex has recognized that the fight for LGBTQ rights is interconnected with other social justice movements, such as racial justice and women's rights. By forming alliances with organizations that address these issues, Vex has expanded the movement's reach and impact. For example, collaborating with local racial justice organizations has led to joint campaigns that highlight the unique challenges faced by LGBTQ people of color.

Leveraging Media and Technology has proven essential in expanding the movement's visibility. Vex has utilized social media platforms to amplify LGBTQ voices, share personal stories, and mobilize support for various initiatives. The viral nature of online campaigns has allowed for rapid dissemination of information, raising awareness about LGBTQ issues on a global scale.

Examples of Impact

The impact of Vex Aleron's efforts to expand the LGBTQ rights movement is evident in several key initiatives:

The Kaevin Pride Parade serves as a prime example of successful activism. This event not only celebrated LGBTQ identities but also raised awareness about the ongoing struggles faced by the community. The parade attracted thousands of participants and supporters, showcasing the strength and diversity of the LGBTQ community in Kaevin. Additionally, it provided a platform for local artists and activists to share their stories, fostering a sense of unity and purpose.

Educational Programs designed by Vex have also made a significant impact. By partnering with schools and community organizations, Vex has developed workshops that educate individuals about LGBTQ history, rights, and issues. These programs have helped to reduce stigma and promote understanding among non-LGBTQ individuals, creating a more inclusive environment.

Legislative Advocacy has resulted in tangible changes in Kaevin's policies. Vex's efforts to engage with local lawmakers have led to the introduction of bills aimed at protecting LGBTQ rights, such as anti-discrimination laws and measures to improve access to healthcare for LGBTQ individuals. These legislative victories demonstrate the effectiveness of sustained advocacy and coalition building.

Conclusion

Expanding the LGBTQ rights movement requires a multifaceted approach that addresses the complexities of identity, challenges internal and external barriers, and employs effective strategies for mobilization and advocacy. Through their leadership and dedication, Vex Aleron has exemplified the spirit of this expansion, inspiring others to join the fight for equality. As the movement continues to evolve, it is imperative that activists remain vigilant, adaptive, and committed to inclusivity, ensuring that the rights of all LGBTQ individuals are recognized and upheld.

Love, Relationships, and Activism

Finding Love in the Midst of Activism

In the whirlwind of activism, where the stakes are high and the battles seem unending, the pursuit of love can often feel like a secondary concern. However, for Vex Aleron, finding love amidst the chaos of LGBTQ activism became a profound aspect of their journey. This section explores the intersection of love and activism, highlighting the complexities, challenges, and ultimately, the beauty that emerges when personal relationships intertwine with the fight for equality.

The Intersection of Love and Activism

Activism demands a significant portion of one's emotional and physical energy. It requires passion, commitment, and often, a willingness to sacrifice personal time for the greater good. In this context, the emergence of romantic relationships can

LOVE, RELATIONSHIPS, AND ACTIVISM

be both a source of strength and a potential distraction. According to [?], love is a transformative force that can enhance one's capacity for activism, providing emotional resilience and support. Vex's experience exemplifies this theory, as love became a catalyst for deeper engagement in their advocacy work.

Challenges in Balancing Activism and Relationships

Despite the potential benefits, finding love while engaged in activism is fraught with challenges. The demanding nature of activism can lead to time constraints, emotional exhaustion, and a sense of isolation. Vex often found themselves torn between attending crucial meetings and spending quality time with their partner. This conflict is not uncommon among activists, as noted by [?], who observed that many activists struggle to maintain personal relationships due to the intensity of their commitments.

For Vex, one of the significant challenges was the fear of vulnerability. Engaging in activism often necessitates a certain level of emotional armor, which can hinder genuine connections. The fear of exposing their true self, both as an activist and a partner, created a barrier that took time to dismantle. Overcoming this barrier required open communication and mutual understanding, emphasizing the importance of vulnerability in relationships, as discussed by [?].

Finding Support in Shared Values

A pivotal moment in Vex's relationship was the realization that their partner shared a commitment to LGBTQ rights. This shared value system not only strengthened their bond but also created a unique partnership where both individuals could support each other's activism. Research by [?] suggests that relationships built on shared values and goals tend to be more resilient, particularly in the face of external pressures.

Vex and their partner often collaborated on initiatives, blending their personal and activist lives. This collaboration fostered a deeper understanding of each other's passions and struggles, reinforcing their relationship. As they navigated the complexities of activism together, they found solace in knowing they were not alone in their fight.

The Role of Community in Nurturing Love

In the LGBTQ community, love often extends beyond romantic partnerships to encompass friendships and chosen families. Vex discovered that their network of fellow activists provided a supportive environment that nurtured their relationship.

This community acted as a buffer against the external pressures of activism, offering encouragement and understanding.

The importance of community support in relationships is echoed in the work of [?], who posits that social networks significantly impact individual well-being and relationship satisfaction. Vex's experience illustrated this theory, as their friends and fellow activists celebrated their relationship milestones, reinforcing the notion that love is a communal experience.

Lessons Learned from Love and Activism

Through their journey of finding love amidst activism, Vex learned several valuable lessons. First and foremost, they discovered the importance of prioritizing self-care. Engaging in activism can be all-consuming, but nurturing a relationship requires intentional effort and time. Vex began to allocate specific moments for their partner, recognizing that love flourishes when given the attention it deserves.

Moreover, Vex learned the significance of open communication. Discussing feelings, fears, and expectations became a cornerstone of their relationship. This transparency not only strengthened their bond but also allowed them to navigate the complexities of activism together. As highlighted by [?], effective communication is crucial in maintaining healthy relationships, particularly in high-stress environments.

Conclusion: Love as a Source of Strength

Ultimately, Vex Aleron's experience underscores the idea that love can serve as a powerful source of strength in the realm of activism. It provides emotional support, enhances resilience, and fosters a sense of belonging in an often tumultuous landscape. As Vex continued to fight for LGBTQ rights, they did so with the knowledge that love—both romantic and platonic—was an integral part of their journey.

In navigating the complexities of love and activism, Vex Aleron not only found a partner but also a fellow warrior in the battle for equality, illustrating that amidst the struggle, love can thrive and inspire change.

Balancing Personal and Professional Life

In the whirlwind of activism, where the fires of passion often burn brightly, the challenge of balancing personal and professional life becomes paramount. For Vex Aleron, this balancing act was not merely a matter of time management, but a complex interplay of identity, relationships, and the demands of being a public figure in the LGBTQ rights movement.

Theoretical Framework

To understand the dynamics of balancing personal and professional life, we can draw upon several theories from organizational behavior and psychology. One prominent theory is the **Work-Life Balance Theory**, which posits that individuals strive to maintain a harmonious relationship between their work and personal lives. This balance is essential for overall well-being and productivity. The theory suggests that when individuals feel overwhelmed in one area, it can lead to stress and decreased performance in the other.

Another relevant framework is the **Role Theory**, which examines how individuals navigate multiple roles in their lives—such as activist, student, friend, and partner. According to this theory, the ability to fulfill these roles effectively depends on the resources available to the individual, including time, energy, and social support.

Challenges Faced

Vex faced numerous challenges in attempting to maintain this delicate balance. The demands of activism often required long hours of work, attending meetings, organizing events, and engaging with the community. This commitment could easily encroach on personal time, leading to feelings of guilt and inadequacy when personal relationships suffered as a result.

Example: The Toll on Relationships For instance, during the preparation for the first Kaevin Pride Parade, Vex found themselves consumed by the logistics of the event. Late nights spent coordinating with vendors and volunteers left little time for personal relationships. One significant relationship that began to strain was with a close friend, Alex, who felt neglected and unappreciated. This situation exemplifies the common problem of **relationship neglect**—where the demands of professional life overshadow personal connections.

Strategies for Balance

To counteract these challenges, Vex implemented several strategies aimed at achieving a more sustainable balance between their activist pursuits and personal life.

1. **Setting Boundaries**   One of the first steps Vex took was to establish clear boundaries between work and personal time. This involved setting specific hours for activism-related activities and committing to unplugging from work during designated personal time. For example, Vex decided that Sundays would be reserved for self-care and socializing with friends, creating a much-needed respite from the pressures of activism.

2. **Prioritizing Relationships**   Vex also learned the importance of prioritizing relationships. By scheduling regular check-ins with friends and loved ones, Vex ensured that personal connections remained strong despite the demands of their activism. This practice not only reinforced their support network but also provided a necessary emotional outlet.

3. **Mindfulness and Self-Care**   Incorporating mindfulness practices into their daily routine became another vital strategy for Vex. Engaging in activities such as meditation, yoga, and journaling helped Vex manage stress and maintain a sense of clarity. These practices allowed Vex to reconnect with their personal identity outside of activism, fostering a sense of balance.

Case Study: The Impact of Balance on Activism

Research has shown that maintaining a balance between personal and professional life can enhance overall effectiveness in activism. A study conducted by Smith and Jones (2020) found that activists who prioritized self-care and personal relationships reported higher levels of satisfaction and commitment to their causes. This finding aligns with Vex's experience, as they noticed that when they felt fulfilled in their personal life, they were more energized and motivated in their activism.

Conclusion

Ultimately, the journey of balancing personal and professional life is an ongoing process, one that requires constant reflection and adjustment. For Vex Aleron, the struggle to find equilibrium between their passionate pursuit of LGBTQ rights and the nurturing of personal relationships became a defining aspect of their activism. By implementing strategies to set boundaries, prioritize relationships, and engage in self-care, Vex not only enhanced their effectiveness as an activist but also enriched their personal life, proving that one does not have to sacrifice the other in the pursuit of equality and justice.

The Power of LGBTQ Love Stories

LGBTQ love stories hold a profound significance in the tapestry of human experience. They serve not only as narratives of personal connection but also as powerful instruments for social change. In a world where traditional love stories have dominated the cultural landscape, LGBTQ love stories challenge norms, inspire empathy, and foster understanding. This section explores the multifaceted impact of LGBTQ love stories on individuals and society, while addressing the theoretical underpinnings, challenges, and notable examples that illustrate their power.

Theoretical Framework

At the heart of LGBTQ love stories lies the concept of narrative identity, as articulated by theorists such as [?]. Narrative identity refers to the internalized and evolving story of the self that individuals construct to make sense of their experiences. For LGBTQ individuals, love stories often become a critical part of this narrative identity, providing a framework through which they can articulate their desires, struggles, and triumphs.

Moreover, queer theory, as posited by [?], emphasizes the fluidity of identity and the performative nature of gender and sexuality. LGBTQ love stories often defy binary categorizations, showcasing the complexity and diversity of love beyond heterosexual norms. This theoretical lens allows for a deeper understanding of how these stories challenge societal expectations and contribute to the broader discourse on love and relationships.

Challenges Faced by LGBTQ Love Stories

Despite their power, LGBTQ love stories encounter numerous challenges, including societal stigma, misrepresentation, and lack of visibility. Many LGBTQ narratives have historically been marginalized or erased, leading to a scarcity of authentic representations in mainstream media. This absence can perpetuate harmful stereotypes and foster a sense of isolation among LGBTQ individuals.

Furthermore, the intersectionality of race, class, and gender within LGBTQ love stories adds layers of complexity. [?] highlights the importance of recognizing how overlapping identities can shape experiences of love and belonging. For instance, LGBTQ individuals of color may face unique challenges that differ from those of their white counterparts, complicating the narrative of love and acceptance.

Examples of Impactful LGBTQ Love Stories

Numerous LGBTQ love stories have made significant cultural impacts, resonating with audiences and inspiring activism. One notable example is the film *Moonlight* (2016), which tells the story of a young Black man grappling with his identity and sexuality while navigating the complexities of love. The film's portrayal of vulnerability and intimacy challenges conventional narratives and invites viewers to empathize with the characters' struggles.

Another powerful example is the novel *Call Me by Your Name* by André Aciman, which captures the essence of first love between two young men in Italy. This story exemplifies the beauty and pain of love, emphasizing the importance of memory and longing in shaping one's identity. The success of the film adaptation further illustrates the demand for authentic LGBTQ narratives in mainstream media.

The Role of Love Stories in Activism

LGBTQ love stories serve as catalysts for activism by humanizing the experiences of marginalized communities. By sharing personal narratives, individuals can challenge societal prejudices and foster understanding among broader audiences. The act of storytelling becomes a form of resistance against erasure and discrimination.

For example, the *It Gets Better* project, initiated in response to the bullying of LGBTQ youth, harnesses the power of personal love stories and affirmations. By sharing their journeys, individuals contribute to a collective narrative that emphasizes hope, resilience, and the possibility of a brighter future.

Conclusion

In conclusion, LGBTQ love stories are not merely tales of romance; they are vital expressions of identity, resilience, and community. By challenging societal norms and fostering empathy, these narratives play a crucial role in the ongoing struggle for LGBTQ equality. As we continue to amplify these stories, we must recognize their power to inspire change, foster connections, and ultimately transform the world into a more inclusive and loving place.

Encouraging Healthy Relationships in the Community

In the vibrant tapestry of LGBTQ activism, the significance of nurturing healthy relationships within the community cannot be overstated. It is essential to understand that healthy relationships are foundational to individual well-being and collective strength. This section delves into the theoretical underpinnings, common challenges faced by LGBTQ individuals, and practical strategies to promote such relationships.

Theoretical Framework

The concept of healthy relationships can be analyzed through several theoretical lenses, including attachment theory, social exchange theory, and the minority stress model.

Attachment Theory posits that early relationships with caregivers shape one's ability to form secure connections in adulthood. For LGBTQ individuals, who may experience rejection or lack of support from their families, fostering secure attachments becomes crucial. This theory suggests that individuals with secure attachments are more likely to engage in positive relational behaviors, such as effective communication and conflict resolution.

Social Exchange Theory suggests that individuals weigh the costs and benefits of their relationships. In the context of LGBTQ relationships, external societal pressures can skew this balance, leading to unhealthy dynamics. By providing resources and support, communities can help individuals recognize the intrinsic value of their relationships beyond societal judgments.

Minority Stress Model elucidates the unique stressors faced by LGBTQ individuals, including stigma, discrimination, and internalized homophobia. These stressors can adversely affect relationship dynamics, making it imperative to create supportive environments that mitigate these challenges.

Common Challenges in LGBTQ Relationships

Despite the richness of LGBTQ relationships, various challenges can hinder their development:

Internalized Homophobia often manifests as self-doubt and negative self-perception, which can lead to difficulties in establishing intimate connections. For instance, an individual who struggles with their sexual orientation may push away potential partners due to fear of rejection or inadequacy.

Societal Stigma can create barriers to forming healthy relationships. Discrimination and prejudice from society may lead to isolation, which in turn affects emotional availability and trust. For example, a gay couple may face hostility from their families or communities, leading to stress that permeates their relationship.

Communication Barriers often arise from differing experiences and expectations. For instance, a transgender individual may find it challenging to communicate their needs to a partner who lacks understanding of gender identity issues.

Strategies for Encouraging Healthy Relationships

To combat these challenges and promote healthy relationships within the LGBTQ community, several strategies can be implemented:

Education and Workshops are vital in equipping individuals with the skills necessary for healthy relationships. Programs focusing on communication, conflict resolution, and understanding diverse identities can empower community members. For example, workshops that include role-playing scenarios can help participants practice effective communication in a safe environment.

Support Groups serve as a vital resource for individuals seeking connection and understanding. These groups can provide a platform for sharing experiences and fostering empathy. For instance, a support group for LGBTQ youth can help participants navigate the complexities of dating and relationships, reinforcing the idea that they are not alone in their experiences.

Mentorship Programs can pair younger LGBTQ individuals with experienced mentors who can offer guidance and support. This relationship can provide a safe space for discussing relationship challenges and developing healthy coping strategies.

Promoting Positive Representation in media and art is essential for normalizing healthy LGBTQ relationships. By showcasing diverse and positive portrayals of love and partnership, communities can inspire individuals to seek out and cultivate similar relationships in their own lives. For instance, films that highlight the struggles and triumphs of LGBTQ couples can serve as both inspiration and a catalyst for conversation.

Fostering Inclusivity within existing community structures is paramount. This can include creating spaces where individuals feel safe to express their identities and seek support. For example, community centers that host LGBTQ-friendly events can provide a welcoming environment for individuals to connect and build relationships.

Real-World Examples

Several initiatives demonstrate effective strategies for fostering healthy relationships within the LGBTQ community:

The Trevor Project offers crisis intervention and suicide prevention services to LGBTQ youth, emphasizing the importance of connection and support. Their outreach programs often include discussions on healthy relationships, helping young individuals navigate their romantic lives with confidence.

PFLAG (Parents, Families, and Friends of Lesbians and Gays) provides a platform for families to learn about LGBTQ identities and how to support their loved ones. By fostering understanding within families, PFLAG helps create a supportive environment that encourages healthy relationships.

Local Pride Organizations often host events focused on relationship-building, such as workshops on communication and love languages. These events not only educate but also create a sense of community, reinforcing the idea that healthy relationships are a shared goal.

Conclusion

Encouraging healthy relationships within the LGBTQ community is a multifaceted endeavor that requires a combination of education, support, and representation. By addressing the unique challenges faced by LGBTQ individuals and implementing targeted strategies, communities can foster an environment where love and connection thrive. As Vex Aleron and fellow activists continue to advocate for equality, the promotion of healthy relationships remains a vital component of their mission, ensuring that all individuals can experience the joy and fulfillment that comes from loving and supportive connections.

Supporting LGBTQ Youth in Romantic Relationships

The journey of LGBTQ youth in navigating romantic relationships can be fraught with unique challenges and complexities. As they explore their identities and seek love and companionship, it is essential to provide them with the necessary support and guidance to foster healthy and fulfilling relationships. This section delves into the significance of supporting LGBTQ youth in their romantic endeavors, the common issues they face, and the strategies that can be employed to empower them.

Understanding the Unique Challenges

LGBTQ youth often encounter a myriad of challenges that can complicate their romantic relationships. These challenges can be categorized into several key areas:

- **Societal Stigma:** Many LGBTQ youth face societal stigma and discrimination, which can lead to feelings of isolation and low self-esteem. This stigma can manifest in various forms, including bullying, harassment, and rejection from peers, family, and community members. Research shows that LGBTQ youth are at a higher risk of experiencing mental health issues, including anxiety and depression, as a result of societal pressures [1].

- **Family Acceptance:** Family dynamics play a crucial role in the lives of LGBTQ youth. Those who experience rejection or lack of support from their families may struggle to form healthy romantic relationships. A study by Ryan et al. (2009) highlights that family acceptance significantly correlates with positive mental health outcomes and healthier relationships for LGBTQ youth.

- **Internalized Homophobia:** Internalized homophobia can lead LGBTQ youth to doubt their self-worth and question their right to love and be loved. This internal conflict can hinder their ability to engage fully in romantic relationships, often leading to fear of vulnerability and intimacy [2].

- **Lack of Role Models:** The absence of positive LGBTQ role models in media and society can leave youth feeling disconnected and uncertain about their relationship dynamics. Without representation, they may struggle to envision what healthy LGBTQ relationships look like, leading to unrealistic expectations and potential relationship difficulties.

Strategies for Support

To effectively support LGBTQ youth in their romantic relationships, a multi-faceted approach is necessary. Here are several strategies that can be employed:

- **Creating Safe Spaces:** Schools, community centers, and other organizations should strive to create safe spaces where LGBTQ youth can express themselves without fear of judgment or discrimination. Safe spaces encourage open discussions about love, relationships, and identity, allowing youth to share their experiences and seek advice in a supportive environment.

- **Promoting Education and Awareness:** Educating LGBTQ youth about healthy relationship dynamics is crucial. Workshops and seminars that focus on communication skills, consent, and emotional intelligence can empower youth to build strong, respectful relationships. Additionally, educating peers and adults about LGBTQ issues can foster a more inclusive environment.

- **Encouraging Family Engagement:** Engaging families in conversations about LGBTQ identities and relationships can help bridge gaps in understanding. Family support programs that offer resources, counseling, and workshops can facilitate acceptance and open lines of communication between LGBTQ youth and their families.

- **Providing Access to Resources:** Access to LGBTQ-friendly counseling and support services can be invaluable for youth navigating romantic relationships. These services can help youth address issues such as internalized homophobia, relationship conflicts, and mental health challenges.

- **Highlighting Positive Role Models:** Showcasing positive LGBTQ relationships through media, literature, and community events can provide youth with relatable examples of love and partnership. Celebrating diverse expressions of love and commitment can inspire youth to embrace their identities and seek healthy relationships.

Real-World Examples

Several organizations and initiatives have successfully implemented strategies to support LGBTQ youth in their romantic relationships:

- **The Trevor Project:** This organization provides crisis intervention and suicide prevention services to LGBTQ youth. They offer resources focused on relationship health, including online guides that address common relationship issues faced by LGBTQ youth.

- **GLSEN:** The Gay, Lesbian and Straight Education Network (GLSEN) works to create safe and affirming schools for LGBTQ youth. Their programs include peer support groups and educational resources that promote understanding of healthy relationships among students.

- **PFLAG:** PFLAG (Parents, Families, and Friends of Lesbians and Gays) provides support for families of LGBTQ individuals. Their resources help families understand LGBTQ identities and foster acceptance, ultimately supporting youth in their romantic relationships.

Conclusion

Supporting LGBTQ youth in their romantic relationships is a critical aspect of fostering their overall well-being and development. By understanding the unique challenges they face and implementing effective support strategies, we can empower these youth to build healthy, fulfilling relationships. As society continues to evolve toward greater acceptance and understanding, it is imperative that we remain vigilant in our efforts to support LGBTQ youth in all facets of their lives, including love and companionship.

Bibliography

[1] Meyer, I. H. (2003). Prejudice, Social Stress, and Mental Health in Gay Men. *American Psychologist,* 58(5), 123-134.

[2] Herek, G. M. (1990). Gender and Sexual Prejudice. *Journal of Interpersonal Violence,* 5(3), 320-331.

[3] Ryan, C., Huebner, D., Diaz, R. M., & Sanchez, J. (2009). Family Rejection as a Predictor of Negative Mental Health Outcomes in White and Latino Lesbian, Gay, and Bisexual Young Adults. *Pediatrics,* 123(1), 346-352.

International Influence

Advocating for LGBTQ Equality Abroad

In an increasingly globalized world, the fight for LGBTQ equality transcends borders, demanding a concerted effort from activists, organizations, and allies worldwide. Advocating for LGBTQ rights abroad involves addressing complex cultural, legal, and social challenges that differ from one nation to another. This section explores the theoretical frameworks, prevailing issues, and practical examples of international LGBTQ advocacy.

Theoretical Frameworks

The advocacy for LGBTQ equality abroad can be framed within several theoretical perspectives, including:

- **Human Rights Theory:** This theory posits that all individuals, regardless of their sexual orientation or gender identity, are entitled to fundamental human rights. The Universal Declaration of Human Rights (UDHR) serves as a foundational document that advocates for the inherent dignity and equality of all people. Article 2 of the UDHR states:

Everyone is entitled to all the rights and freedoms set forth in this Declaration, without

(14)

This principle is crucial in framing LGBTQ advocacy as a human rights issue rather than a cultural or moral debate.

- **Intersectionality:** Coined by Kimberlé Crenshaw, this framework emphasizes the interconnected nature of social categorizations such as race, class, and gender, which create overlapping systems of discrimination or disadvantage. In the context of LGBTQ advocacy, intersectionality highlights the unique challenges faced by LGBTQ individuals who also belong to marginalized racial, ethnic, or socioeconomic groups.

- **Globalization and Transnationalism:** These theories examine how global interconnectedness shapes social movements. LGBTQ advocacy is increasingly influenced by transnational networks that facilitate the sharing of resources, strategies, and solidarity across borders. This interconnectedness allows for a more unified approach to combating global homophobia and transphobia.

Challenges in LGBTQ Advocacy Abroad

Despite the theoretical frameworks supporting LGBTQ rights, numerous challenges persist in advocating for equality on a global scale:

- **Cultural Resistance:** Many societies hold deeply ingrained cultural beliefs that oppose LGBTQ rights. Activists often face significant backlash from conservative factions that view LGBTQ advocacy as a threat to traditional values. For instance, in countries like Uganda and Nigeria, anti-LGBTQ legislation is often justified by appeals to cultural and religious norms.

- **Legal Barriers:** In many countries, LGBTQ individuals face criminalization based on their sexual orientation or gender identity. Laws against homosexuality can lead to severe penalties, including imprisonment or violence. For example, in Saudi Arabia, homosexuality is punishable by death, creating a perilous environment for LGBTQ individuals.

- **Lack of Resources:** Many LGBTQ organizations operating in low-income countries struggle with limited funding and resources, hindering their ability to effectively advocate for change. This scarcity can stifle grassroots movements and limit the reach of international support.

- **Political Repression:** In some regions, governments actively suppress LGBTQ advocacy through censorship, intimidation, and violence. Activists in countries like Russia have faced crackdowns on pride events and public demonstrations, creating a climate of fear that stifles activism.

Practical Examples of Advocacy

Despite these challenges, numerous organizations and activists have made significant strides in advocating for LGBTQ equality abroad:

- **International LGBTQ Organizations:** Groups like ILGA (International Lesbian, Gay, Bisexual, Trans and Intersex Association) and OutRight Action International work tirelessly to promote LGBTQ rights on a global scale. These organizations provide resources, support, and advocacy tools to local activists, fostering a sense of solidarity and shared purpose.

- **Grassroots Movements:** Local activists often lead the charge for change. In Brazil, the Grupo Gay da Bahia has been instrumental in raising awareness about violence against LGBTQ individuals and advocating for legal reforms. Their efforts have contributed to the recognition of LGBTQ rights within Brazilian law.

- **Diplomatic Engagement:** Some countries have begun to incorporate LGBTQ rights into their foreign policy. For example, the United States has established the Global Equality Fund, which supports LGBTQ rights initiatives worldwide. This fund provides grants to organizations working to combat discrimination and promote equality.

- **Cultural Exchange Programs:** Programs that foster cultural exchange can play a vital role in LGBTQ advocacy. By facilitating dialogue and understanding between different cultures, these initiatives can challenge stereotypes and promote acceptance. The U.S. State Department's International Visitor Leadership Program, which brings international leaders to the U.S. for exchanges, has included LGBTQ activists to share their experiences and strategies.

Conclusion

Advocating for LGBTQ equality abroad is a multifaceted endeavor that requires a nuanced understanding of cultural, legal, and social contexts. By employing theoretical frameworks such as human rights theory, intersectionality, and transnationalism, activists can effectively navigate the complexities of global advocacy. While challenges such as cultural resistance, legal barriers, and political repression persist, the resilience and determination of LGBTQ activists worldwide continue to inspire hope and drive change. As the movement for equality evolves, it is essential to recognize the interconnectedness of global struggles and the importance of solidarity in the fight for LGBTQ rights.

Addressing Global Homophobia and Transphobia

In the contemporary landscape of LGBTQ activism, addressing global homophobia and transphobia has emerged as a critical component of the movement. The persistence of discriminatory laws and social stigma against LGBTQ individuals worldwide presents a multifaceted challenge that activists like Vex Aleron have sought to confront head-on. This section explores the theoretical frameworks, problems, and examples of efforts to combat these pervasive issues.

Theoretical Frameworks

To effectively address global homophobia and transphobia, it is essential to understand the underlying theories that inform activism. One prominent framework is *Intersectionality*, coined by Kimberlé Crenshaw, which posits that individuals experience oppression in varying degrees based on their intersecting identities, including race, gender, sexual orientation, and socioeconomic status. This theory highlights that solutions must be tailored to consider the unique experiences of marginalized groups within the LGBTQ community.

Another critical theory is *Queer Theory*, which challenges the binary understanding of gender and sexuality. It advocates for the deconstruction of normative frameworks that perpetuate discrimination. By applying queer theory, activists can create inclusive spaces that recognize and celebrate the diversity of gender identities and sexual orientations, thereby fostering a more comprehensive approach to combating global homophobia and transphobia.

Problems Faced

Despite the progress made in some regions, global homophobia and transphobia remain entrenched in many societies. The following problems illustrate the scope of these issues:

1. **Legal Discrimination**: In numerous countries, laws criminalizing homosexuality and gender non-conformity continue to exist. For instance, in countries like Uganda and Nigeria, harsh penalties, including imprisonment and violence, are imposed on LGBTQ individuals. These legal frameworks not only perpetuate stigma but also embolden societal discrimination.

2. **Cultural Stigma**: Deep-rooted cultural beliefs often exacerbate homophobia and transphobia. Many societies view LGBTQ identities as deviant or immoral, leading to ostracization and violence against individuals. This cultural stigma is reinforced by religious doctrines that condemn non-heteronormative relationships.

3. **Lack of Representation**: The absence of LGBTQ voices in political and media spheres hampers progress toward equality. Without representation, the narratives surrounding LGBTQ individuals are often shaped by those who do not understand their experiences, perpetuating harmful stereotypes and misinformation.

4. **Violence and Harassment**: LGBTQ individuals face heightened risks of violence, including hate crimes and domestic abuse. According to the International Lesbian, Gay, Bisexual, Trans and Intersex Association (ILGA), a significant percentage of LGBTQ individuals report experiencing violence due to their sexual orientation or gender identity.

Examples of Activism

Activists like Vex Aleron have employed various strategies to combat global homophobia and transphobia, drawing inspiration from successful movements worldwide:

1. **International Advocacy**: Collaborating with global organizations such as ILGA and Human Rights Campaign, activists work to pressure governments to repeal discriminatory laws and adopt inclusive policies. For example, the "Free and Equal" campaign launched by the United Nations aims to promote equal rights and acceptance for LGBTQ individuals globally.

2. **Grassroots Movements**: Local grassroots organizations play a pivotal role in addressing homophobia and transphobia. In many regions, these organizations provide support services, legal aid, and advocacy training to

empower LGBTQ individuals. For instance, the "LGBTQ Rights Initiative" in Eastern Europe focuses on community building and awareness campaigns to challenge societal norms.

3. **Cultural Change Initiatives**: Activists are also leveraging art, media, and education to shift cultural perceptions. The "It Gets Better" project, which began as a response to the alarming rates of suicide among LGBTQ youth, has become a global phenomenon, sharing positive narratives and fostering hope.

4. **Digital Activism**: The rise of social media has transformed the landscape of activism. Campaigns like #LoveIsLove and #TransRightsAreHumanRights have garnered international attention, mobilizing support and raising awareness about LGBTQ issues. These digital platforms allow activists to connect with a broader audience, share resources, and amplify marginalized voices.

Conclusion

Addressing global homophobia and transphobia requires a multifaceted approach that considers legal, cultural, and societal factors. By employing theoretical frameworks such as intersectionality and queer theory, activists like Vex Aleron can develop strategies that are inclusive and effective. The ongoing struggle against discrimination calls for solidarity among activists worldwide, as they work together to dismantle oppressive systems and advocate for the rights of LGBTQ individuals everywhere. As the movement evolves, it is crucial to remain vigilant and proactive in combating the pervasive issues of homophobia and transphobia, ensuring that the fight for equality continues across borders and cultures.

Establishing Alliance with International Activists

In the ever-evolving landscape of LGBTQ rights, the significance of establishing alliances with international activists cannot be overstated. As Vex Aleron's journey unfolded, it became increasingly clear that the fight for equality transcended borders, cultures, and languages. This realization propelled Vex into a realm of global activism, where collaboration and solidarity became essential tools in the quest for justice.

Theoretical Framework

The foundation for building international alliances rests on the principles of *solidarity* and *intersectionality*. Solidarity emphasizes a collective responsibility among activists to support one another, recognizing that the struggles faced by LGBTQ individuals in one country often mirror those in another.

INTERNATIONAL INFLUENCE

Intersectionality, a term coined by Kimberlé Crenshaw, highlights the interconnected nature of social categorizations such as race, class, and gender, which can create overlapping systems of discrimination. By embracing these frameworks, Vex aimed to foster a comprehensive understanding of the global LGBTQ landscape.

Challenges in Establishing Alliances

Despite the noble intentions behind international collaboration, several challenges emerged. One significant issue was the *cultural differences* that often led to misunderstandings. Activists from different regions brought unique perspectives shaped by their local contexts, which sometimes resulted in conflicting approaches to advocacy. For example, while some activists focused on legal reforms, others prioritized grassroots movements. Bridging these gaps required patience, empathy, and a willingness to engage in open dialogue.

Another challenge was the *political climate* in various countries. In some regions, LGBTQ activists faced severe repression, making it difficult to establish connections with those in more progressive areas. Vex encountered stories of activists who had been imprisoned or exiled for their work, underscoring the risks involved in international solidarity. This reality necessitated a cautious approach, ensuring that alliances did not put individuals in harm's way.

Examples of Successful Alliances

Despite these challenges, Vex successfully forged alliances with international activists through strategic initiatives. One notable example was the collaboration with the *International LGBTQ Rights Coalition*, which aimed to unify activists across borders. By organizing virtual summits and workshops, Vex and fellow activists shared best practices, resources, and strategies for effective advocacy. These gatherings not only strengthened individual movements but also created a sense of global community.

Additionally, Vex participated in the *Global Pride Conference*, where activists from diverse backgrounds came together to discuss pressing issues. This event highlighted the power of storytelling, as participants shared personal narratives that resonated across cultures. Vex utilized these stories to advocate for a more inclusive approach to LGBTQ rights, emphasizing that while the struggles may differ, the desire for equality is universal.

The Role of Technology

The advent of technology played a pivotal role in establishing international alliances. Social media platforms became essential tools for activists to connect, share information, and mobilize support. Vex harnessed the power of platforms like Twitter and Instagram to amplify voices from marginalized communities worldwide. By creating hashtags such as `#GlobalLGBTQUnity`, Vex facilitated conversations that transcended geographical boundaries, fostering a sense of belonging among activists.

Moreover, online campaigns allowed for rapid dissemination of information, enabling activists to respond swiftly to emerging issues. For instance, when a wave of anti-LGBTQ legislation swept through several countries, Vex coordinated a global day of action, urging supporters to raise awareness and advocate for change. The immediate response showcased the effectiveness of international solidarity in combating injustice.

Future Directions

As Vex Aleron continued to navigate the complexities of international activism, the focus shifted toward sustaining these alliances. Recognizing that the fight for LGBTQ rights is an ongoing struggle, Vex emphasized the importance of long-term relationships built on trust and mutual respect. Future initiatives included mentorship programs that paired seasoned activists with emerging leaders from different countries, ensuring the transfer of knowledge and experiences.

Furthermore, Vex advocated for the establishment of a *Global LGBTQ Rights Fund*, aimed at providing financial support for grassroots movements in regions facing systemic oppression. By pooling resources and sharing expertise, activists could strengthen their efforts and enhance their impact on a global scale.

In conclusion, establishing alliances with international activists proved to be a transformative aspect of Vex Aleron's journey. By embracing solidarity, navigating challenges, and leveraging technology, Vex not only expanded the reach of LGBTQ advocacy but also contributed to a more interconnected and resilient global movement for equality. The path ahead remains fraught with obstacles, but the power of collective action continues to illuminate the way forward in the ongoing fight for LGBTQ rights worldwide.

Sharing Best Practices and Strategies

In the pursuit of LGBTQ equality, sharing best practices and strategies among activists and organizations is crucial. This collaborative approach not only enhances the effectiveness of campaigns but also fosters a sense of community and solidarity among diverse groups. The following sections outline key theories, challenges, and successful examples that illustrate the importance of sharing knowledge in the LGBTQ rights movement.

Theoretical Framework

The framework of *Collective Impact* serves as a foundational theory for sharing best practices in activism. According to Kania and Kramer (2011), Collective Impact is a structured approach to collaboration that involves five key conditions: 1. **Common Agenda:** All participants must have a shared vision for change. 2. **Shared Measurement Systems:** Participants agree on how success will be measured and reported. 3. **Mutually Reinforcing Activities:** Each participant's efforts must align with the overarching goals. 4. **Continuous Communication:** Open dialogue is essential for building trust and ensuring alignment. 5. **Backbone Support Organizations:** A dedicated group must coordinate the efforts of all participants.

By applying this framework, LGBTQ activists can effectively share strategies and resources, leading to a more unified and impactful movement.

Challenges in Sharing Practices

While the benefits of sharing best practices are clear, several challenges can hinder this process: - **Fragmentation:** The LGBTQ movement is diverse, encompassing various identities, cultures, and experiences. This diversity can lead to fragmentation, where different groups may prioritize distinct issues, making it difficult to establish a common agenda. - **Resource Disparities:** Not all organizations have equal access to resources, including funding, training, and technology. This disparity can create barriers to participation in collaborative efforts. - **Communication Gaps:** Differences in language, terminology, and communication styles can lead to misunderstandings and hinder effective collaboration.

To overcome these challenges, it is essential to establish clear communication channels and create inclusive spaces where all voices are heard.

Successful Examples of Knowledge Sharing

Several organizations and initiatives have successfully implemented strategies for sharing best practices in the LGBTQ rights movement:

1. **The Human Rights Campaign (HRC):** HRC has developed a comprehensive toolkit for LGBTQ advocacy that includes resources on legal rights, community organizing, and public education. By providing these materials online, HRC enables activists across the country to access and adapt proven strategies to their local contexts.

2. **The Trevor Project:** This organization focuses on crisis intervention and suicide prevention among LGBTQ youth. The Trevor Project shares best practices through training programs for educators and community leaders, equipping them with the tools to support LGBTQ youth effectively. Their *Trevor Lifeline* service exemplifies the importance of sharing knowledge on mental health resources.

3. **Global LGBTQ Networks:** Organizations like ILGA (International Lesbian, Gay, Bisexual, Trans and Intersex Association) facilitate the sharing of strategies across borders. By connecting activists from different countries, ILGA promotes the exchange of successful advocacy techniques and creates a global dialogue on LGBTQ rights.

Practical Strategies for Sharing Best Practices

To enhance collaboration and knowledge sharing, LGBTQ activists can adopt the following practical strategies:

- **Workshops and Training Sessions:** Hosting regular workshops allows activists to share their experiences and learn from one another. These sessions can cover topics such as grassroots organizing, digital activism, and community engagement.

- **Online Platforms and Social Media:** Utilizing social media platforms to share successes, challenges, and resources can reach a broader audience. Creating dedicated hashtags or groups can facilitate ongoing discussions and resource sharing.

- **Mentorship Programs:** Establishing mentorship programs can connect experienced activists with newcomers. This relationship fosters knowledge transfer and encourages the development of new leaders within the movement.

- **Collaborative Campaigns:** Engaging in joint campaigns with other organizations can amplify messages and resources. By pooling efforts, activists can tackle larger issues and create a more significant impact.

Conclusion

Sharing best practices and strategies is vital for the success of the LGBTQ rights movement. By fostering collaboration, overcoming challenges, and learning from successful examples, activists can strengthen their efforts and create a more inclusive and equitable society. As the movement continues to evolve, the commitment to sharing knowledge will be essential in the ongoing fight for LGBTQ equality, ensuring that all voices are heard and valued.

Making an Impact on a Global Scale

In an increasingly interconnected world, the fight for LGBTQ rights transcends borders, prompting activists like Vex Aleron to engage with global issues. This section explores the multifaceted ways in which Vex and their peers have made significant contributions to the international LGBTQ rights movement, addressing both the challenges and successes encountered along the way.

Theoretical Framework

The global LGBTQ rights movement can be understood through the lens of *Transnational Advocacy Networks* (TANs), as proposed by Keck and Sikkink (1998). These networks consist of various actors, including NGOs, activists, and international organizations, who collaborate across borders to influence policy and public opinion. Vex's activism exemplifies this theory, as they built alliances with international organizations to amplify their message and create a unified front against discrimination.

Addressing Global Homophobia and Transphobia

One of the primary challenges faced by LGBTQ activists globally is the persistent prevalence of homophobia and transphobia, often rooted in cultural, religious, and political contexts. For instance, in many countries, laws criminalizing same-sex relationships continue to exist, perpetuating violence and discrimination. Vex's advocacy work included campaigns aimed at raising awareness about these issues, highlighting stories of individuals affected by such laws, and using social media platforms to spread these narratives.

$$\text{Impact} = \frac{\text{Awareness} \times \text{Engagement}}{\text{Resistance}} \tag{15}$$

This equation illustrates the dynamics at play; as awareness and engagement increase, the impact of activism grows, albeit tempered by the resistance faced from entrenched societal norms.

Establishing Alliances with International Activists

Vex recognized the importance of collaboration in the fight for LGBTQ rights. They attended international conferences and workshops, where they connected with activists from diverse backgrounds. These interactions not only provided Vex with new strategies and insights but also fostered a sense of solidarity among activists. For example, Vex collaborated with activists from Eastern Europe, where anti-LGBTQ sentiment is particularly strong, to share resources and strategies for grassroots mobilization.

Sharing Best Practices and Strategies

Through their engagement with international activists, Vex learned the importance of adapting strategies to fit local contexts. They emphasized the need for culturally sensitive approaches, understanding that what works in one region may not be effective in another. This adaptability is crucial in addressing the unique challenges faced by LGBTQ communities worldwide.

For instance, Vex participated in a workshop on *community organizing* in South America, where they learned about the power of storytelling in mobilizing support. Inspired by this, Vex initiated a campaign in Kaevin that encouraged local LGBTQ individuals to share their stories, thereby humanizing the struggle for rights and fostering empathy within the broader community.

Making an Impact through Global Campaigns

Vex's activism also extended to participating in global campaigns such as *International Day Against Homophobia, Transphobia, and Biphobia* (IDAHOT). By organizing events in Kaevin, they not only raised awareness locally but also contributed to a larger global movement. These events included educational workshops, art exhibitions, and public demonstrations that united diverse groups in the fight for equality.

$$\text{Global Impact} = \sum_{i=1}^{n} \text{Local Actions}_i \times \text{Global Awareness}_i \qquad (16)$$

Here, the equation represents the cumulative effect of local actions, each multiplied by the level of global awareness they generate, illustrating how localized efforts can contribute to a broader impact.

Making a Lasting Impact

Ultimately, Vex's efforts in the global LGBTQ rights movement underscore the importance of sustained engagement and collaboration. By leveraging their experiences and building upon the work of others, Vex has not only made a significant impact in Kaevin but has also contributed to the global dialogue surrounding LGBTQ rights. Their journey illustrates that while challenges remain, the collective efforts of activists worldwide can lead to meaningful change.

In conclusion, Vex Aleron's commitment to LGBTQ activism on a global scale exemplifies the interconnectedness of the struggle for equality. By addressing local issues while engaging with international movements, Vex has played a pivotal role in shaping a more inclusive future for LGBTQ individuals everywhere.

The Price of Activism

Dealing with Burnout and Mental Health Challenges

In the whirlwind of activism, burnout emerges as a formidable adversary, often lurking in the shadows of passion and commitment. For Vex Aleron, the relentless pursuit of LGBTQ rights in Kaevin was both a source of strength and a breeding ground for mental health challenges. Understanding burnout requires a multifaceted approach, encompassing psychological, sociological, and physiological perspectives.

Understanding Burnout

Burnout is characterized by emotional exhaustion, depersonalization, and a diminished sense of personal accomplishment [1]. The World Health Organization (WHO) recognizes it as an occupational phenomenon, which can be exacerbated in high-stakes environments like activism. The cyclical nature of activism, where victories are often followed by new battles, can lead to an overwhelming sense of fatigue.

$$\text{Burnout} = \text{Emotional Exhaustion} + \text{Depersonalization} + \text{Reduced Accomplishment} \tag{17}$$

Vex experienced this equation firsthand. The emotional toll of witnessing discrimination and injustice took a heavy toll on their spirit, leading to feelings of inadequacy and isolation. In high-pressure situations, the need to remain resilient can overshadow the need for self-care, creating a precarious balance.

The Impact on Mental Health

The mental health implications of burnout are profound. Vex often found themselves grappling with anxiety and depression, common companions in the life of an activist. The American Psychological Association (APA) highlights that chronic stress can lead to long-term psychological issues, including PTSD, particularly for those who are constantly fighting against systemic oppression [2].

$$\text{Mental Health} = \text{Emotional Well-Being} + \text{Psychological Resilience} + \text{Social Support} \tag{18}$$

In Vex's journey, the decline in mental health was evident. The lack of emotional well-being and the struggle for psychological resilience were compounded by the absence of adequate social support, especially during moments of defeat. The stigma surrounding mental health in many activist circles often prevented open discussions about these challenges, further isolating individuals like Vex.

Identifying the Signs of Burnout

Recognizing the signs of burnout is crucial for prevention and recovery. Vex learned to identify key indicators, such as:

- Chronic fatigue and lack of energy
- Increased cynicism or negativity towards activism
- Difficulty concentrating or making decisions
- Withdrawal from social interactions and support networks
- Feelings of helplessness and hopelessness

By acknowledging these symptoms, Vex began to understand that burnout was not a personal failure but a common experience among activists. This shift in perspective allowed for a more compassionate approach to self-care.

Coping Strategies

To combat burnout, Vex implemented several coping strategies, emphasizing the importance of self-care and community support. These strategies included:

1. **Mindfulness and Meditation:** Engaging in mindfulness practices helped Vex center themselves amidst chaos. Research shows that mindfulness can reduce stress and enhance emotional regulation [3].

$$\text{Mindfulness} = \frac{\text{Attention}}{\text{Judgment}} \qquad (19)$$

2. **Setting Boundaries:** Learning to say no and prioritize personal well-being became essential. Vex recognized that taking on too many responsibilities could lead to increased stress and decreased effectiveness in activism.

3. **Seeking Professional Help:** Therapy provided Vex with tools to navigate the complexities of their mental health. Engaging with mental health professionals allowed for the exploration of feelings in a safe environment.

4. **Building a Support Network:** Surrounding themselves with like-minded individuals who shared similar experiences fostered a sense of belonging. This network provided emotional support and practical advice, creating a buffer against the stresses of activism.

5. **Engaging in Creative Outlets:** Vex found solace in art and writing, using creative expression as a therapeutic tool. Engaging in activities that brought joy and fulfillment helped alleviate feelings of burnout.

Conclusion

Dealing with burnout and mental health challenges is an ongoing journey for activists like Vex Aleron. By recognizing the signs, implementing coping strategies, and fostering a supportive community, the path to recovery becomes more navigable. As Vex continued to fight for LGBTQ rights in Kaevin, they learned that prioritizing mental health was not a sign of weakness but a crucial element of sustained activism. The fight for equality is not just about the external battles; it is equally about nurturing the internal landscape of resilience and well-being.

Bibliography

[1] Maslach, C., & Jackson, S. E. (1981). *The measurement of experienced burnout.* Journal of Organizational Behavior, 2(2), 99-113.

[2] American Psychological Association. (2018). *Stress in America: Generation Z.* Retrieved from https://www.apa.org/news/press/releases/stress/2018/stress-gen-z.pdf

[3] Kabat-Zinn, J. (1990). *Full Catastrophe Living: Using the Wisdom of Your Body and Mind to Face Stress, Pain, and Illness.* Delacorte Press.

The Toll on Personal Relationships

In the journey of activism, the personal relationships of individuals like Vex Aleron often bear the brunt of the emotional and physical demands that come with fighting for LGBTQ rights. The toll on personal relationships can manifest in various forms, including emotional distance, strain on friendships, and challenges in romantic partnerships. This section delves into the complexities and dynamics of personal relationships that activists face, supported by relevant theories and real-world examples.

Emotional Distance and Isolation

Activism can be an all-consuming endeavor, leading to emotional distance from loved ones. According to the *Attachment Theory* (Bowlby, 1969), secure attachments are crucial for healthy relationships. However, when one becomes absorbed in activism, the time and energy that should be devoted to nurturing these bonds can dwindle.

For instance, Vex found that as their commitment to organizing the first Kaevin Pride Parade intensified, they began to miss family gatherings and social events with friends. This absence created a rift, leading to feelings of isolation.

Friends expressed concern, noting that Vex seemed preoccupied and less available for emotional support. This scenario illustrates how the demands of activism can inadvertently lead to a neglect of personal relationships, resulting in emotional withdrawal.

Strain on Friendships

The strain on friendships can also be exacerbated by differing levels of commitment to social justice. Activists may encounter friends who do not share the same passion or urgency for LGBTQ rights, leading to feelings of frustration and disappointment. This phenomenon can be explained through the *Social Identity Theory* (Tajfel & Turner, 1979), which posits that individuals derive part of their identity from the groups they belong to.

As Vex's involvement in the LGBTQ rights movement deepened, they found themselves gravitating towards like-minded individuals, while friendships with those less engaged began to wane. For example, a once-close friendship with a childhood friend faltered when that friend expressed discomfort with Vex's outspoken activism. Vex felt that their values were being challenged, leading to a painful but necessary decision to distance themselves from that friendship.

Challenges in Romantic Partnerships

Romantic relationships can also suffer under the weight of activism. The *Dual Process Model* (Stroebe & Schut, 1999) suggests that individuals must balance emotional processing with practical coping strategies during stressful times. For activists, this balance can be particularly challenging.

Vex's romantic relationship with Alex, another activist, initially flourished due to their shared commitment to the cause. However, as the pressures of activism mounted, they faced difficulties in maintaining their connection. The constant demands of organizing events, attending meetings, and dealing with backlash left little time for nurturing their relationship. They found themselves arguing more frequently, often about trivial matters, as the stress of their activism spilled over into their personal lives.

Navigating Conflict and Reconciliation

Conflict resolution becomes vital in preserving personal relationships impacted by activism. The *Interest-Based Relational Approach* (Fisher & Ury, 1981) emphasizes the importance of maintaining relationships while addressing conflicts. Vex and

Alex learned to apply this approach by prioritizing open communication and actively listening to each other's needs.

For instance, after a particularly heated argument about their differing roles in the activism, Vex initiated a heart-to-heart conversation. They expressed their feelings of being overwhelmed and acknowledged Alex's frustrations about feeling neglected. This honest dialogue allowed them to realign their priorities, ensuring that their relationship remained a source of support rather than a point of contention.

The Role of Community Support

Community support plays a crucial role in mitigating the toll of activism on personal relationships. Engaging with supportive networks can provide emotional resources that help activists navigate the challenges they face. Vex found solace in attending LGBTQ support groups, where they could share their experiences and receive validation from others who understood the unique pressures of activism.

Moreover, these communities often provide opportunities for socializing and forming new friendships, helping to fill the gaps left by strained relationships. Vex's participation in these groups not only offered emotional relief but also introduced them to new allies and friends who shared their passion for activism, thereby enriching their social life.

Conclusion

In conclusion, the toll on personal relationships is a significant aspect of the activist experience. Emotional distance, strain on friendships, and challenges in romantic partnerships can all arise as individuals like Vex Aleron dedicate themselves to the fight for LGBTQ rights. However, through effective conflict resolution, the support of the community, and a commitment to maintaining open communication, activists can navigate these challenges and preserve the vital connections that sustain them in their journey for equality.

Facing Legal Retribution and Harassment

In the tumultuous landscape of LGBTQ activism, the path to equality is often fraught with legal challenges and personal harassment. Activists like Vex Aleron, while striving for justice, frequently find themselves in the crosshairs of a system that can be both oppressive and retaliatory. This section explores the multifaceted nature of legal retribution and harassment faced by LGBTQ activists, examining the theoretical frameworks, real-world implications, and illustrative examples that encapsulate these struggles.

Theoretical Framework

At its core, the legal challenges faced by LGBTQ activists can be understood through the lens of Critical Legal Studies (CLS), which posits that law is not a neutral arbiter but a tool of power used to maintain the status quo. This perspective highlights how laws can be manipulated to suppress marginalized voices, particularly those advocating for LGBTQ rights. For instance, anti-LGBTQ legislation often emerges under the guise of "protecting traditional values," thereby legitimizing discrimination and harassment.

Furthermore, the concept of *structural violence*, as articulated by Johan Galtung, provides insight into the systemic nature of harassment faced by LGBTQ activists. Structural violence refers to harm inflicted through social structures rather than direct physical violence, manifesting in discriminatory laws, social stigma, and institutionalized homophobia. This framework helps elucidate the insidious ways in which legal systems can perpetuate inequality.

Legal Challenges

In Kaevin, Vex Aleron encountered a myriad of legal obstacles as he championed LGBTQ rights. One notable example was the introduction of a local ordinance aimed at curbing protests that were deemed "disruptive." While ostensibly neutral, this ordinance disproportionately affected LGBTQ activists, who often relied on public demonstrations to voice their concerns. Vex and his allies argued that such laws were a form of legal retribution, designed to silence dissent and maintain the status quo.

Legal retribution can also take the form of harassment through the judicial system itself. Activists may face frivolous lawsuits intended to intimidate and exhaust their resources. For instance, Vex was once served with a lawsuit claiming defamation for his public statements against a local hate group. This tactic, known as *strategic lawsuits against public participation* (SLAPP), aims to deter activists from speaking out by burdening them with legal fees and the stress of litigation.

Personal Harassment

Beyond legal challenges, Vex faced personal harassment that threatened his safety and well-being. As an outspoken advocate, he became a target for online harassment, including threats and doxxing—where personal information is maliciously shared online. Such harassment is not merely a byproduct of activism; it is a calculated strategy employed by opponents to instill fear and silence voices advocating for change.

The psychological toll of facing harassment is profound. Research indicates that activists who experience such harassment may suffer from increased levels of anxiety, depression, and post-traumatic stress disorder (PTSD). For Vex, the constant threat of harassment led to sleepless nights and a pervasive sense of vulnerability, despite his outward bravado.

Building Resilience

In response to these challenges, Vex and his fellow activists developed strategies to build resilience against legal retribution and harassment. One effective approach was the establishment of legal defense funds, which provided financial support for activists facing lawsuits. These funds not only alleviated the financial burden but also fostered a sense of community and solidarity among activists.

Additionally, Vex emphasized the importance of mental health resources for activists. Recognizing the emotional strain of activism, he advocated for workshops and support groups focused on coping strategies and resilience-building. By prioritizing mental health, Vex and his peers created a more sustainable model of activism that could withstand the pressures of legal and personal harassment.

Conclusion

Facing legal retribution and harassment is an unfortunate reality for many LGBTQ activists, including Vex Aleron. Through theoretical frameworks like Critical Legal Studies and the concept of structural violence, we can better understand the systemic challenges that activists encounter. By sharing personal experiences and developing resilience strategies, activists can navigate these treacherous waters and continue their fight for equality, inspiring future generations to stand firm against oppression.

In the end, the battle for LGBTQ rights is not just about legal victories but about the courage to persist in the face of adversity. Vex Aleron's journey serves as a testament to the strength of the human spirit and the unwavering quest for justice, regardless of the obstacles that lie ahead.

Staying Grounded amidst Success and Fame

In the tumultuous landscape of activism, where the bright lights of recognition can easily overshadow the core mission, staying grounded amidst success and fame is both a challenge and a necessity. For Vex Aleron, the rise to prominence in the LGBTQ rights movement in Kaevin came with its own set of complexities. Success, while often celebrated, can lead to feelings of isolation, pressure, and a disconnect from the very community one seeks to uplift.

One theoretical framework that can help us understand the phenomenon of maintaining one's authenticity in the face of fame is the *Social Identity Theory* (Tajfel & Turner, 1979). This theory posits that individuals derive a sense of self from their group memberships. For Vex, the LGBTQ community served as a foundational element of identity. However, as fame began to eclipse personal life, the challenge became how to reconcile the public persona with the private individual.

The Pressure of Public Scrutiny

As Vex's activism gained traction, the media spotlight intensified. Public appearances and interviews became frequent, and with them came the pressure to represent the LGBTQ community flawlessly. This pressure often breeds a phenomenon known as *imposter syndrome*, where individuals doubt their accomplishments and fear being exposed as a "fraud." Vex experienced this firsthand, grappling with the constant scrutiny of both supporters and detractors. The need to appear perfect can lead to a dissonance between one's true self and the persona projected to the world.

To combat this, Vex adopted several strategies:

- **Mindfulness Practices**: Engaging in mindfulness and meditation helped Vex stay connected to personal values and the community's needs. Mindfulness encourages a focus on the present moment, reducing anxiety about public perception.

- **Authentic Relationships**: Surrounding oneself with trusted friends and mentors who provided honest feedback proved invaluable. These relationships acted as a buffer against the isolating effects of fame.

- **Community Engagement**: Vex prioritized grassroots involvement, reminding oneself of the movement's core purpose. Participating in community events and listening to the voices of those directly affected by discrimination helped ground Vex in reality.

Balancing Personal and Professional Life

The line between personal and professional life blurred as Vex's activism gained momentum. The demands of leadership often encroached on personal time, leading to burnout. The *Work-Life Balance Theory* suggests that individuals must find equilibrium between professional responsibilities and personal well-being (Greenhaus & Allen, 2011). For Vex, this balance was crucial to maintaining mental health and effectiveness as an activist.

To achieve this balance, Vex implemented:

- **Setting Boundaries**: Establishing clear boundaries between work and personal time allowed Vex to recharge. Scheduling "no-work" periods became essential for mental health.

- **Self-Care Routines**: Regular self-care practices, including physical exercise and creative outlets, helped mitigate stress and maintain emotional well-being. Engaging in art and music not only provided an escape but also reinforced Vex's commitment to the community.

- **Delegation**: Recognizing the importance of teamwork, Vex learned to delegate responsibilities within the activist organization. This not only alleviated personal pressure but also empowered other leaders within the community.

Community Support and Accountability

In a world where success can lead to alienation, Vex found strength in community support. The LGBTQ community is rich with diverse voices and experiences, providing a network of accountability. Engaging with this community allowed Vex to stay connected to the movement's grassroots origins.

- **Peer Support Groups**: Vex participated in peer-led support groups, where activists could share experiences and strategies for coping with the pressures of fame. These gatherings fostered a sense of belonging and mutual understanding.

- **Mentorship Programs**: By mentoring younger activists, Vex not only contributed to the community but also gained perspective on the evolving landscape of LGBTQ rights. This role reinforced the idea that activism is a collective effort, not an individual endeavor.

- **Public Accountability**: Vex embraced transparency regarding personal challenges and failures. By openly discussing struggles, Vex fostered a culture of honesty within the activist community, encouraging others to seek help and support.

Reflection and Growth

Finally, regular reflection on personal values and goals became a cornerstone of Vex's journey. Engaging in self-reflection practices, such as journaling and guided meditation, allowed for a deeper understanding of the relationship between personal identity and public persona.

Utilizing the *Reflective Practice Model* (Schön, 1983), Vex assessed experiences to inform future actions. This model emphasizes the importance of learning from both successes and setbacks, fostering continuous personal growth.

$$\text{Learning} = \text{Experience} + \text{Reflection} \tag{20}$$

By embracing this formula, Vex transformed challenges into opportunities for development, ensuring that success did not eclipse the fundamental mission of advocating for LGBTQ rights in Kaevin.

In conclusion, the journey through success and fame is fraught with challenges, but with the right strategies and support, it is possible to remain grounded. Vex Aleron's commitment to authenticity, community engagement, and personal well-being underscores the importance of staying true to oneself amidst the chaos of public life. In the end, it is this authenticity that resonates most deeply with the community and fuels the ongoing fight for equality.

Finding Strength in Community Support

In the tumultuous journey of LGBTQ activism, finding strength in community support is not just beneficial; it is essential. The LGBTQ community has long been characterized by resilience, solidarity, and a shared history of struggle against oppression. This section delves into the theoretical frameworks surrounding community support, the challenges faced by activists, and the transformative power of collective action.

Theoretical Frameworks

Community support can be understood through several theoretical lenses, including Social Identity Theory and the Theory of Collective Action.

Social Identity Theory posits that individuals derive a sense of self from their group memberships. For LGBTQ individuals, identifying with a community can foster a sense of belonging and validation. This is crucial in combating feelings of isolation that often accompany marginalization. Research indicates that strong social identities can enhance psychological well-being, particularly in minority groups [2].

Theory of Collective Action suggests that individuals are more likely to engage in activism when they perceive a shared identity and collective efficacy. Collective efficacy refers to the belief that a group can work together to achieve a common goal. This belief is foundational in mobilizing individuals towards activism, as it reinforces the idea that together, they can effect change [?].

Challenges Faced by Activists

Despite the inherent strength found in community support, LGBTQ activists often encounter significant challenges. These include:

Burnout and Mental Health Struggles: The emotional labor involved in activism can lead to burnout. Activists frequently face high levels of stress, anxiety, and depression, exacerbated by external pressures such as societal discrimination and internal community conflicts. A study by [1] found that LGBTQ activists reported higher levels of mental health issues compared to their heterosexual counterparts, highlighting the need for supportive networks.

Isolation within the Community: Ironically, while community support is vital, activists can sometimes feel isolated even within their own communities. Differences in identity—such as race, gender identity, and socioeconomic status—can create divisions. For example, LGBTQ people of color may experience unique challenges that are not always recognized by their white counterparts, leading to feelings of alienation [?].

Examples of Community Support in Action

Numerous examples illustrate the power of community support in fostering resilience among LGBTQ activists:

Peer Support Networks: Organizations such as The Trevor Project and GLSEN provide vital resources and support for LGBTQ youth. They create safe spaces where individuals can share their experiences and seek guidance. The impact of such networks is profound; studies show that youth who engage with supportive peers report higher self-esteem and lower rates of suicidal ideation [?].

Collective Events and Gatherings: Events like Pride parades and community forums serve as powerful reminders of solidarity. These gatherings not only celebrate identity but also reinforce community ties. For instance, the annual Kaevin Pride Parade became a unifying event, drawing thousands together in a show of strength and resilience. Participants reported feeling empowered and supported, which is crucial for maintaining motivation in activism.

Digital Activism and Online Communities: In the digital age, social media platforms have become vital spaces for community support. Online groups provide a platform for sharing resources, organizing events, and offering emotional support. For example, the hashtag #LoveIsLove became a rallying cry for LGBTQ rights, fostering a sense of global community and solidarity.

Conclusion

Finding strength in community support is a cornerstone of LGBTQ activism. Through shared identities, collective action, and robust support networks, activists can navigate the challenges of their journey. By fostering environments where individuals feel valued and connected, the LGBTQ community can continue to inspire resilience and drive meaningful change.

Chapter 3

Political Engagement

Running for Local Office

In the vibrant tapestry of Kaevin's political landscape, Vex Aleron stood at the crossroads of personal ambition and communal responsibility. The decision to run for local office was not merely a career move; it was a declaration of intent, a bold statement that resonated with the aspirations of many marginalized voices within the community. The journey began with a realization that true change requires more than passionate protests and eloquent speeches; it necessitates a seat at the table where decisions are made.

The Decision to Run

The decision to run for local office emerged from a confluence of personal experiences and the pressing needs of the LGBTQ community. Vex understood that representation matters. The absence of openly queer individuals in local governance perpetuated a cycle of neglect, where policies were crafted without considering the unique challenges faced by LGBTQ citizens. The theory of *descriptive representation* posits that constituents benefit when their representatives mirror their identities. Vex's candidacy was a response to this theory, aiming to bridge the gap between the community's needs and the political apparatus.

Challenges in the Campaign

Running for office, however, was not without its challenges. Vex faced a plethora of obstacles, ranging from internal doubts to external opposition. The initial hurdle was the pervasive fear of homophobia within the political sphere. Many LGBTQ individuals have historically been marginalized in politics, leading to a reluctance to engage in the electoral process. Vex had to confront this fear head-on, crafting a campaign that emphasized inclusivity and unity rather than division.

Moreover, the campaign was fraught with logistical challenges. Organizing a grassroots movement required significant resources—time, money, and volunteers. Vex employed the theory of *resource mobilization*, which emphasizes the importance of mobilizing resources to achieve social change. Fundraising events, community outreach, and leveraging social media became essential components of the campaign strategy. For instance, Vex organized a series of town hall meetings that not only educated the electorate about LGBTQ issues but also provided a platform for community members to voice their concerns.

Engaging with the Electorate

A critical aspect of Vex's campaign was the emphasis on engagement. Vex believed that a successful campaign must resonate with the electorate's values and concerns. This involved extensive canvassing efforts, where Vex and volunteers knocked on doors, engaged in conversations, and listened to the constituents' needs. Vex's approach was grounded in the theory of *deliberative democracy*, which advocates for inclusive dialogue as a means of fostering understanding and participation in the political process.

Through these interactions, Vex discovered that many constituents were not only concerned about LGBTQ issues but also about broader social justice topics, such as economic inequality and access to healthcare. This insight allowed Vex to craft a platform that addressed the intersectionality of these issues, appealing to a wider audience while maintaining a strong focus on LGBTQ rights.

Overcoming Opposition

As the campaign gained momentum, Vex encountered opposition from conservative factions within Kaevin. These groups often resorted to fear-mongering tactics, attempting to discredit Vex's candidacy by perpetuating stereotypes and misinformation about the LGBTQ community. Vex's response was rooted in resilience and strategic communication. By reframing the narrative and emphasizing shared values—such as community safety and prosperity—Vex effectively countered the negative rhetoric.

Additionally, Vex utilized the theory of *framing*, which involves presenting issues in a way that resonates with the audience's beliefs and values. By framing LGBTQ rights as fundamental human rights, Vex was able to broaden the appeal of the campaign and garner support from allies who may not have previously identified as LGBTQ advocates.

Victory and Its Implications

The culmination of Vex's efforts came on election day, marked by a palpable sense of anticipation within the community. The victory was not just a personal achievement; it represented a seismic shift in Kaevin's political landscape. Vex's election to local office signified a breakthrough for LGBTQ representation, inspiring a new generation of activists and leaders.

The implications of this victory extended beyond Vex's personal journey. It served as a beacon of hope for marginalized communities, demonstrating that change is possible through perseverance and dedication. Vex's success reinforced the importance of representation in governance, illustrating that diverse voices are essential in shaping policies that reflect the needs of all citizens.

In conclusion, Vex Aleron's journey to running for local office encapsulates the essence of grassroots activism and the transformative power of representation. By navigating the complexities of the political landscape with courage and tenacity, Vex not only carved a path for themselves but also laid the groundwork for future leaders in the ongoing fight for LGBTQ equality in Kaevin.

Defying Political Traditions

In the landscape of Kaevin politics, where tradition often dictated the boundaries of acceptable discourse and representation, Vex Aleron emerged as a beacon of change. Defying entrenched political norms, Vex's candidacy for local office was not merely a personal ambition; it represented a seismic shift in the political culture of a society that had long been resistant to progressive ideas, particularly those concerning LGBTQ rights.

Challenging the Status Quo

Vex's approach to politics was rooted in a fundamental challenge to the status quo. Traditional political figures in Kaevin often adhered to conservative ideologies, prioritizing the interests of the majority while marginalizing minority voices. This created an environment where LGBTQ issues were relegated to the periphery, often dismissed as irrelevant or too controversial for serious discussion. Vex understood that to truly advocate for equality, one must first confront and dismantle these outdated paradigms.

To illustrate this, consider the case of the Kaevin City Council meetings prior to Vex's involvement. These meetings were characterized by a lack of representation and a reluctance to address LGBTQ concerns. For instance, in a 2018 council meeting, a proposal to implement anti-discrimination policies was met with resistance from several council members who argued that such measures were unnecessary and would infringe upon the rights of other citizens. Vex's candidacy sought to challenge these assertions head-on, advocating for policies that recognized the dignity and rights of all individuals, regardless of their sexual orientation or gender identity.

Building a Diverse Coalition

Recognizing the importance of coalition-building, Vex actively sought to engage with various community groups that had historically been sidelined in political discourse. This included not only LGBTQ organizations but also groups representing women, people of color, and individuals with disabilities. By fostering an inclusive dialogue, Vex aimed to create a political platform that resonated with a broad spectrum of constituents.

The concept of coalition politics is well-documented in political theory. According to *Theories of Political Coalitions* by David Stasavage, successful coalitions are built on shared interests and mutual benefits, allowing diverse groups to unite for a common cause. Vex exemplified this theory in practice, as evidenced by the formation of the *Kaevin Alliance for Equality*, a coalition that brought together various advocacy groups to promote LGBTQ rights alongside other social justice issues.

Innovative Campaign Strategies

Vex's campaign strategy was a radical departure from traditional methods employed by political candidates in Kaevin. While most candidates relied heavily on established networks and fundraising from affluent donors, Vex harnessed the power of grassroots mobilization and social media to amplify their message. This approach not only democratized the campaign process but also resonated with younger voters who felt disillusioned by conventional political practices.

A notable example of this innovative strategy was the use of social media platforms to engage voters directly. Vex launched a campaign hashtag, #KaevinForAll, which quickly gained traction, encouraging constituents to share their stories and experiences related to LGBTQ discrimination. This not only humanized the issues at stake but also created a sense of community among supporters, showcasing the collective strength of marginalized voices.

Facing Political Resistance

Despite the momentum Vex generated, the path to political office was fraught with challenges. Traditionalists within the political establishment reacted defensively to Vex's candidacy, often resorting to smear campaigns and attempts to undermine their credibility. For instance, during a televised debate, Vex faced pointed questions about their qualifications and commitment to traditional values, which were framed as being incompatible with the needs of the broader community.

However, Vex's resilience in the face of such adversity was a testament to their commitment to change. Drawing on the theoretical framework of *Resilience Theory*, which posits that individuals and communities can withstand and adapt to challenges, Vex demonstrated that political resistance could be transformed into a rallying cry for supporters. Their ability to articulate a vision of inclusivity and equality resonated deeply with voters, ultimately leading to a groundswell of support that transcended traditional political boundaries.

Legacy of Change

Vex Aleron's defiance of political traditions in Kaevin not only paved the way for their own candidacy but also inspired a new generation of activists and leaders. By challenging the norms that had long governed political discourse, Vex created a legacy that emphasized the importance of representation and inclusivity in governance.

The impact of Vex's efforts can be measured in the subsequent elections, where a record number of LGBTQ candidates emerged, each bringing their unique perspectives and experiences to the political arena. This phenomenon aligns with the *Descriptive Representation Theory*, which suggests that increased representation of marginalized groups leads to better policy outcomes and a more equitable society.

In conclusion, Vex Aleron's journey in defying political traditions serves as a powerful reminder of the potential for change within entrenched systems. By challenging the status quo, building diverse coalitions, employing innovative strategies, and demonstrating resilience in the face of resistance, Vex not only altered the political landscape of Kaevin but also ignited a movement that continues to inspire activists around the world. The fight for LGBTQ equality is ongoing, but the groundwork laid by Vex and their allies ensures that the future is brighter for all who dare to challenge tradition.

Championing LGBTQ Rights in Kaevin's Government

In the vibrant political landscape of Kaevin, Vex Aleron emerged as a formidable advocate for LGBTQ rights, navigating the complexities of local governance while championing equality and inclusion. This section explores Vex's strategies, challenges, and triumphs in advocating for LGBTQ rights within the governmental framework of Kaevin.

Understanding the Political Landscape

To effectively champion LGBTQ rights, it was crucial for Vex to understand the political landscape of Kaevin. The local government was characterized by a mix of progressive and conservative elements, creating a challenging environment for LGBTQ advocacy. Vex recognized that successful advocacy required not only passion but also a strategic approach grounded in political theory.

Political theorist John Rawls' concept of *justice as fairness* provided a framework for Vex's advocacy. According to Rawls, a just society is one in which individuals have equal rights and opportunities, and inequalities are arranged to benefit the least advantaged. Vex applied this principle by advocating for policies that would elevate the rights and visibility of marginalized LGBTQ individuals in Kaevin.

Building Alliances

Vex understood that championing LGBTQ rights required building coalitions with like-minded politicians and community organizations. By forming alliances with progressive members of the local council, Vex was able to amplify the voice of the LGBTQ community. This collaborative approach was essential in navigating the often contentious political debates surrounding LGBTQ rights.

For instance, Vex collaborated with the *Kaevin Equality Coalition*, a grassroots organization dedicated to advocating for LGBTQ rights. Together, they organized community forums to raise awareness about LGBTQ issues, fostering dialogue between constituents and elected officials. These forums served as a platform for sharing personal stories, highlighting the need for inclusive policies, and mobilizing public support.

Legislative Initiatives

Armed with a deep understanding of the political landscape and strong alliances, Vex initiated several legislative proposals aimed at advancing LGBTQ rights in Kaevin. One of the most significant initiatives was the introduction of the *Kaevin Equality Act*, which aimed to prohibit discrimination based on sexual orientation and gender identity in employment, housing, and public accommodations.

The legislative process was fraught with challenges. Vex faced opposition from conservative council members who argued that the proposed legislation infringed upon religious freedoms. To counter this argument, Vex utilized a combination of legal theory and ethical reasoning. Drawing on the principles of *utilitarianism*, Vex articulated that the greatest good for the greatest number would be achieved through the protection of LGBTQ individuals from discrimination.

$$U = \sum_{i=1}^{n} \frac{G_i}{N} \tag{21}$$

Where U represents overall utility, G_i is the benefit to individual i, and N is the total number of individuals affected. By framing the discussion in terms of overall societal benefit, Vex was able to garner support from moderate council members who recognized the importance of inclusivity for the community's well-being.

Engaging the Public

Public engagement played a pivotal role in Vex's advocacy efforts. Understanding that grassroots support was essential for legislative success, Vex launched a comprehensive public awareness campaign titled *Kaevin for All*. This campaign utilized various media platforms, including social media, local radio, and community events, to educate the public about LGBTQ rights and the significance of the proposed legislation.

The campaign featured testimonials from LGBTQ individuals who shared their experiences of discrimination and the impact it had on their lives. By humanizing the issues at stake, Vex successfully mobilized public support, leading to increased attendance at city council meetings and a surge in letters and emails to council members advocating for the passage of the Kaevin Equality Act.

Navigating Challenges and Opposition

Despite the momentum gained through public support, Vex faced significant challenges from organized opposition groups. These groups often employed misinformation and fear tactics to sway public opinion against LGBTQ rights. Vex recognized the importance of addressing these challenges head-on, utilizing both evidence-based arguments and emotional appeals to counteract the negative narratives.

For example, when faced with claims that the Kaevin Equality Act would lead to the erosion of religious freedoms, Vex organized a panel discussion featuring legal experts who explained the protections already in place for religious organizations. This proactive approach not only dispelled myths but also showcased Vex's commitment to fostering an inclusive dialogue around LGBTQ rights.

Achieving Legislative Success

After months of advocacy, coalition-building, and public engagement, the Kaevin Equality Act was finally put to a vote. The culmination of Vex's efforts was met with a mix of anticipation and anxiety. On the day of the vote, Vex stood before the council, armed with a deep understanding of the issues, unwavering resolve, and the support of the community.

The vote was a historic moment for Kaevin, as the council ultimately passed the Kaevin Equality Act with a majority in favor. This landmark legislation not only prohibited discrimination based on sexual orientation and gender identity but also established an LGBTQ advisory board to ensure ongoing representation and advocacy within local governance.

Reflections on Impact

The successful passage of the Kaevin Equality Act marked a significant milestone in Vex's journey as an activist and leader. It demonstrated the power of grassroots advocacy, coalition-building, and strategic engagement in effecting change within the political system. Vex's efforts inspired a new generation of activists in Kaevin, illustrating that championing LGBTQ rights is not only a moral imperative but also an achievable goal within the framework of local governance.

As Vex reflected on this achievement, it became clear that the fight for LGBTQ rights in Kaevin was far from over. The passage of the Kaevin Equality Act was merely the beginning of a broader movement toward equality, inclusion, and justice for all members of the community. Vex's journey continued, fueled by the belief that every individual, regardless of their sexual orientation or gender identity, deserves the right to live authentically and without fear.

In conclusion, Vex Aleron's advocacy for LGBTQ rights within Kaevin's government exemplifies the transformative power of political engagement and community activism. By championing the principles of justice, collaboration, and public engagement, Vex not only advanced LGBTQ rights but also contributed to the ongoing struggle for equality in Kaevin and beyond.

Collaborating with Like-Minded Politicians

In the intricate landscape of political advocacy, collaboration with like-minded politicians emerges as a pivotal strategy for advancing LGBTQ rights. This section delves into the theoretical frameworks underpinning such collaborations, the challenges faced, and notable examples that illustrate effective partnerships in the pursuit of equality.

Theoretical Frameworks

The concept of collaboration in political contexts can be analyzed through various theoretical lenses, including social capital theory and coalition-building frameworks. Social capital theory posits that the relationships and networks among individuals can facilitate collective action for mutual benefit. In the context of LGBTQ activism, politicians who share similar values and goals can leverage their social capital to amplify their voices and create a unified front against discrimination.

Coalition-building frameworks emphasize the importance of forming alliances across different political spectrums to achieve common objectives. This approach is particularly relevant in LGBTQ activism, where intersectional issues often require the collaboration of diverse groups. By aligning with politicians who advocate for human rights, social justice, and equality, LGBTQ activists can create a broader coalition that enhances their impact.

Challenges in Collaboration

Despite the potential benefits of collaborating with like-minded politicians, several challenges can hinder these efforts. One significant issue is the presence of political polarization, which can create barriers to effective communication and collaboration. In environments where LGBTQ rights are contentious, politicians may be hesitant to align themselves with activists due to fear of backlash from their constituents or party members.

Moreover, the diversity of opinions within the LGBTQ community itself can complicate collaboration. Different factions may prioritize various issues, leading to disagreements on strategies and goals. For instance, while some politicians may focus on marriage equality, others might prioritize anti-discrimination laws or healthcare access for LGBTQ individuals. Navigating these differences requires strong leadership and a commitment to finding common ground.

Examples of Successful Collaborations

One notable example of successful collaboration is the partnership between LGBTQ activists and progressive politicians during the campaign for marriage equality in the United States. Figures such as former President Barack Obama and Senator Tammy Baldwin worked closely with grassroots organizations to advocate for the legalization of same-sex marriage. Their collaboration not only brought national attention to the issue but also helped shift public opinion, ultimately leading to the landmark Supreme Court ruling in *Obergefell v. Hodges* (2015).

In Kaevin, a similar collaboration emerged during the push for comprehensive anti-discrimination legislation. Local LGBTQ leaders formed alliances with sympathetic city council members who were committed to promoting equality. Together, they organized town hall meetings, engaged in community outreach, and mobilized constituents to advocate for the proposed legislation. This grassroots effort culminated in the successful passage of the Kaevin Equality Act, which provided robust protections for LGBTQ individuals in employment, housing, and public accommodations.

Strategies for Effective Collaboration

To foster successful collaborations with like-minded politicians, several strategies can be employed:

1. **Building Relationships**: Establishing personal connections with politicians can facilitate open communication and trust. Regular meetings, informal gatherings, and shared experiences can strengthen these relationships.

2. **Shared Goals**: Clearly articulating common objectives is essential. By identifying overlapping interests, activists and politicians can create a focused agenda that resonates with both parties.

3. **Public Engagement**: Joint public events, such as rallies and forums, can showcase the collaboration and draw attention to the cause. These events not only raise awareness but also demonstrate the united front of activists and politicians.

4. **Leveraging Media**: Utilizing media platforms to highlight collaborative efforts can amplify the message and reach a broader audience. Press releases, social

media campaigns, and interviews can effectively communicate the partnership's goals and achievements.

5. **Continuous Dialogue**: Maintaining an ongoing dialogue is crucial for adapting to changing circumstances and addressing emerging challenges. Regular check-ins and updates can ensure that all parties remain aligned and engaged.

Conclusion

Collaborating with like-minded politicians serves as a powerful tool in the struggle for LGBTQ rights. By leveraging social capital, overcoming challenges, and employing effective strategies, activists can create impactful partnerships that drive meaningful change. The examples of successful collaborations in Kaevin and beyond illustrate the potential for collective action to transform political landscapes and promote equality for all.

Passing LGBTQ-Inclusive Legislation

The journey towards passing LGBTQ-inclusive legislation in Kaevin was not merely a political endeavor; it was a reflection of the changing societal attitudes towards sexual and gender minorities. This section explores the theoretical frameworks, challenges, and successful examples that shaped this legislative milestone.

Theoretical Frameworks

To understand the significance of LGBTQ-inclusive legislation, we can draw from several theoretical perspectives:

- **Social Contract Theory:** This theory posits that individuals consent, either explicitly or implicitly, to form a society and be governed. In the context of LGBTQ rights, the social contract must include the acknowledgment of all identities, ensuring that LGBTQ individuals are afforded the same rights and protections as their heterosexual counterparts.

- **Intersectionality:** Coined by Kimberlé Crenshaw, this framework emphasizes that individuals experience multiple, intersecting identities that affect their social experiences and access to rights. Legislation must consider the diverse backgrounds of LGBTQ individuals, including race, gender, and socioeconomic status, to be genuinely inclusive.

- **Human Rights Framework:** LGBTQ-inclusive legislation can be viewed through the lens of human rights, which asserts that all individuals are entitled to certain inalienable rights. The Universal Declaration of Human Rights serves as a foundational document, advocating for equality and non-discrimination.

Challenges Faced

Despite the theoretical backing, the path to passing LGBTQ-inclusive legislation was fraught with challenges:

- **Political Resistance:** Many politicians were reluctant to support LGBTQ rights due to fear of backlash from their constituents or political parties. This resistance often stemmed from deeply ingrained prejudices and misconceptions about LGBTQ individuals.

- **Public Misinformation:** Misinformation about LGBTQ issues proliferated, often perpetuated by conservative media outlets and religious organizations. This misinformation created a hostile environment for legislative discussions, complicating the efforts of activists.

- **Legal Hurdles:** Existing laws often contradicted the principles of equality and non-discrimination. Activists had to navigate a complex legal landscape, challenging outdated laws while advocating for new protections.

Successful Examples of Legislation

Despite these challenges, several key pieces of legislation emerged as milestones in the fight for LGBTQ rights in Kaevin:

- **The Equality Act:** This landmark legislation aimed to prohibit discrimination based on sexual orientation and gender identity in employment, housing, and public accommodations. The passage of the Equality Act was a culmination of years of advocacy and public support, signaling a significant shift in societal attitudes.

- **The Gender Identity Protection Bill:** This bill specifically aimed to protect the rights of transgender and non-binary individuals in various sectors, including healthcare and education. The legislation was informed by extensive research and testimonies from the transgender community, highlighting the urgent need for protections.

- **The Youth Protection Act:** Recognizing the unique challenges faced by LGBTQ youth, this act provided guidelines for schools to create safe and inclusive environments. It mandated anti-bullying policies and established support systems for LGBTQ students, ensuring that they could thrive academically and socially.

The Legislative Process

The process of passing LGBTQ-inclusive legislation involved several key steps:

1. **Grassroots Mobilization:** Activists organized campaigns to raise awareness and garner public support. This included rallies, social media campaigns, and partnerships with local organizations.

2. **Lobbying Efforts:** Engaging with lawmakers through lobbying was crucial. Activists met with legislators, provided them with data and personal stories, and urged them to support the proposed bills.

3. **Public Hearings and Testimonies:** Public hearings allowed community members to voice their support or opposition to the legislation. Testimonies from LGBTQ individuals were particularly impactful, humanizing the issues at stake and emphasizing the need for change.

4. **Coalition Building:** Collaborating with other marginalized groups, such as racial minorities and women's rights organizations, helped to create a united front advocating for equality. This intersectional approach strengthened the overall movement.

Conclusion

Passing LGBTQ-inclusive legislation in Kaevin marked a significant victory in the ongoing struggle for equality. It was a testament to the power of collective action, the importance of theoretical frameworks in shaping policy, and the resilience of a community determined to secure its rights. As Vex Aleron and fellow activists celebrated these legislative victories, they understood that the fight for LGBTQ rights was far from over. Each piece of legislation was not just a law but a step towards a more inclusive and equitable society for all.

Taking on the Media

Challenging Stereotypes and Misrepresentation

The representation of LGBTQ individuals in media and society often falls prey to harmful stereotypes that perpetuate misunderstanding and discrimination. These stereotypes not only mischaracterize LGBTQ identities but also shape public perception and policy. In this section, we will explore the nature of these stereotypes, the impact of misrepresentation, and the strategies employed by activists to challenge these narratives.

Understanding Stereotypes

Stereotypes are oversimplified and generalized beliefs about a group, which can lead to misconceptions and prejudice. According to [?], stereotypes serve as cognitive shortcuts that can simplify the complexities of social identity. However, these shortcuts can often lead to dehumanization and the reinforcement of negative attitudes.

For LGBTQ individuals, common stereotypes include the notion that gay men are effeminate and promiscuous, while lesbian women are often depicted as masculine or unfeminine. Transgender individuals face their own set of stereotypes, often being portrayed as deceptive or mentally ill. These stereotypes are not only inaccurate but also harmful, as they contribute to societal stigmatization and discrimination.

The Impact of Misrepresentation

Misrepresentation in media can have profound effects on the LGBTQ community. Research by [1] indicates that exposure to negative media portrayals can lead to internalized homophobia, where individuals adopt society's negative views about their own sexual orientation. This internalized stigma can result in mental health issues, including anxiety and depression.

Furthermore, misrepresentation can influence public policy. When LGBTQ individuals are depicted negatively in media, it can lead to a lack of support for LGBTQ rights and protections. For example, during the fight for marriage equality in the United States, opponents often relied on stereotypes of gay relationships to argue against legalization, framing them as unstable or harmful to societal norms.

Activism Against Stereotypes

Activists like Vex Aleron have taken a stand against these damaging stereotypes through various means. One effective strategy is the use of counter-narratives that highlight the diverse and authentic experiences of LGBTQ individuals. By sharing personal stories, activists can humanize the community and challenge the oversimplified views perpetuated by mainstream media.

For instance, during the Kaevin Pride Parade, Vex organized a series of workshops that invited LGBTQ individuals to share their stories. These narratives not only provided visibility but also fostered understanding among allies and those outside the community. By showcasing the complexities of LGBTQ lives, activists can dismantle the monolithic portrayals often found in media.

Leveraging Media for Change

To effectively challenge stereotypes, LGBTQ activists have increasingly turned to digital media and social platforms. The rise of social media has provided a space for marginalized voices to share their experiences and advocate for change. Campaigns such as #LoveIsLove and #TransIsBeautiful have gained traction, promoting positive representations and challenging negative stereotypes.

Moreover, the creation of LGBTQ-inclusive media content is essential. Activists have collaborated with filmmakers, writers, and artists to produce works that accurately reflect the diversity of the LGBTQ experience. Shows like *Pose* and *Schitt's Creek* have been praised for their authentic representation of LGBTQ characters, challenging traditional stereotypes and fostering acceptance.

Conclusion

Challenging stereotypes and misrepresentation is a vital aspect of LGBTQ activism. By understanding the harmful effects of stereotypes and employing strategies to counter them, activists like Vex Aleron are making significant strides toward a more inclusive society. The journey is ongoing, but with each story shared and each stereotype dismantled, the path toward equality becomes clearer.

Exposing Media Bias and Homophobia

The media plays a pivotal role in shaping societal attitudes and perceptions regarding LGBTQ individuals and issues. Unfortunately, this influence is often marred by bias and homophobia, which can perpetuate stereotypes and foster discrimination. In this section, we will explore the mechanisms of media bias, the implications of homophobic representations, and the strategies employed to expose and combat these injustices.

Understanding Media Bias

Media bias refers to the perceived or real partiality of journalists and news organizations in the coverage of events, issues, and individuals. This bias can manifest in various forms, including:

- **Selection Bias:** The choice of which stories to cover can reflect a bias towards sensationalism or negativity, particularly regarding LGBTQ topics. For instance, coverage of LGBTQ events may focus disproportionately on conflicts or controversies rather than positive developments or community achievements.

- **Framing:** The way stories are presented can influence public perception. For example, framing LGBTQ rights as a "debate" rather than a matter of human rights can undermine the legitimacy of the community's struggles.

- **Language Use:** The terminology employed in media narratives can carry implicit biases. Terms that pathologize or sensationalize LGBTQ identities contribute to a culture of stigma. For example, referring to LGBTQ individuals as "deviant" or "abnormal" can reinforce negative stereotypes.

Consequences of Homophobic Representation

The consequences of biased media representation are profound and far-reaching. Research indicates that negative portrayals of LGBTQ individuals can lead to increased levels of discrimination and violence against them. According to the *American Psychological Association*, exposure to negative media representations correlates with heightened prejudice and intolerance among viewers.

Moreover, such portrayals can adversely affect the mental health of LGBTQ individuals. The *National Alliance on Mental Illness* reports that LGBTQ youth are at a higher risk for depression and anxiety, often exacerbated by societal stigma. When the media amplifies homophobic narratives, it contributes to a hostile environment that can lead to feelings of isolation and unworthiness among LGBTQ individuals.

Case Studies and Examples

Several high-profile instances illustrate the impact of media bias and homophobia:

- **The Coverage of Same-Sex Marriage:** During the lead-up to the legalization of same-sex marriage in various jurisdictions, media coverage often framed the issue as a contentious debate rather than a civil rights issue. This framing not only polarized public opinion but also marginalized the voices of LGBTQ individuals advocating for their rights.

- **Transgender Representation:** The portrayal of transgender individuals in media has historically been fraught with inaccuracies and sensationalism. For instance, reality television shows often depict transgender individuals in a negative light, focusing on their struggles rather than their achievements. This misrepresentation can perpetuate harmful stereotypes, leading to discrimination in broader society.

Strategies for Exposing Bias

Activists and allies have developed several strategies to expose media bias and combat homophobia:

- **Media Literacy Campaigns:** Educating the public about media bias and encouraging critical consumption of media can empower individuals to recognize and challenge homophobic narratives. Workshops and seminars can be organized to enhance media literacy among LGBTQ youth and their allies.

- **Engaging with Journalists:** Building relationships with journalists and media outlets can create opportunities for advocacy. By providing resources and insights, activists can help reporters understand the complexities of LGBTQ issues and encourage more accurate and respectful coverage.

- **Utilizing Social Media:** Social media platforms serve as powerful tools for exposing bias. Activists can leverage these platforms to highlight instances of homophobia in media, mobilize public support, and demand accountability from media organizations.

Conclusion

Exposing media bias and homophobia is crucial in the ongoing fight for LGBTQ equality. By understanding the mechanisms of bias, recognizing the consequences of negative representation, and implementing effective strategies for advocacy, activists can challenge harmful narratives and foster a more inclusive media landscape. Ultimately, the goal is to create a media environment that reflects the diversity and richness of LGBTQ lives, promoting understanding and acceptance in society at large.

Creating LGBTQ-Inclusive Media Content

In the contemporary landscape of media, representation matters more than ever. Creating LGBTQ-inclusive media content is not just about visibility; it is about authenticity, respect, and the recognition of diverse narratives that challenge the status quo. This section explores the theories behind media representation, the problems faced by LGBTQ creators, and notable examples of successful inclusive content.

Theoretical Framework

The foundation of LGBTQ-inclusive media content can be anchored in several theoretical frameworks. One such framework is the **Representation Theory**, which posits that media representations shape societal perceptions and attitudes towards marginalized groups. According to Hall (1997), representation involves the active construction of meaning, wherein media producers play a crucial role in how LGBTQ identities are portrayed. This theory emphasizes the importance of nuanced and authentic portrayals that reflect the complexity of LGBTQ experiences.

Another relevant theory is **Queer Theory**, which critiques the binary understanding of gender and sexuality. It advocates for the inclusion of non-normative identities and experiences in media narratives. This theory encourages creators to move beyond stereotypes and embrace fluidity in identity representation, allowing for a more comprehensive view of LGBTQ lives.

Challenges in Creating Inclusive Content

Despite the theoretical frameworks advocating for LGBTQ representation, numerous challenges persist in the creation of inclusive media content. One significant issue is the **Gatekeeping** phenomenon, where mainstream media executives often dictate which stories are told and how they are represented. This can lead to a lack of authentic LGBTQ voices in the creative process, resulting in narratives that do not resonate with the actual experiences of LGBTQ individuals.

Moreover, there is a pervasive issue of **Stereotyping** within media portrayals. LGBTQ characters are often confined to clichéd roles, such as the flamboyant gay best friend or the tragic queer figure. Such limited representations can perpetuate harmful stereotypes and fail to capture the diversity within the LGBTQ community.

This not only alienates LGBTQ audiences but also reinforces negative perceptions among non-LGBTQ viewers.

Successful Examples of LGBTQ-Inclusive Content

Despite the challenges, there have been significant strides in the creation of LGBTQ-inclusive media content. A notable example is the television series *Pose*, which focuses on the lives of LGBTQ individuals, particularly Black and Latinx transgender women, during the 1980s and 1990s. The show has been praised for its authentic representation and involvement of LGBTQ creators, including a predominantly LGBTQ cast and crew. This commitment to authenticity has allowed *Pose* to resonate deeply with audiences, providing visibility to marginalized narratives often overlooked in mainstream media.

Another exemplary case is the animated series *Steven Universe*, which has been lauded for its inclusive representation of LGBTQ relationships and identities. The show features a diverse array of characters, including non-binary and queer individuals, and explores themes of love and acceptance. Its creator, Rebecca Sugar, has openly discussed the importance of representation in children's media, emphasizing that inclusive content can foster understanding and empathy among young audiences.

The Role of Social Media and Digital Platforms

The rise of social media and digital platforms has revolutionized the landscape of LGBTQ-inclusive media content. Platforms like YouTube and TikTok have empowered LGBTQ creators to share their stories and perspectives directly with audiences. This democratization of content creation allows for a wider range of narratives, often bypassing traditional media gatekeepers.

For instance, creators such as *Lindsay Ellis* and *ContraPoints* have utilized their platforms to engage in discussions about LGBTQ issues while incorporating humor and critical analysis. Their content not only entertains but also educates audiences about the complexities of LGBTQ identities and experiences.

Conclusion

Creating LGBTQ-inclusive media content is an essential endeavor that requires a commitment to authenticity, representation, and inclusivity. By embracing diverse narratives and challenging stereotypes, media creators can contribute to a more equitable representation of LGBTQ individuals in society. As we move forward, it is imperative to continue advocating for inclusive practices within the media industry, ensuring that all voices are heard and celebrated.

$$\text{Representation} = \text{Visibility} + \text{Authenticity} + \text{Diversity} \quad (22)$$

Constructively Engaging with Critics

Engaging with critics, especially in the realm of LGBTQ activism, is not merely an act of defense but a strategic maneuver that can lead to constructive dialogue and greater understanding. This section explores the theoretical underpinnings of engagement, the common problems faced, and practical examples of how to turn criticism into opportunities for growth and advocacy.

Theoretical Framework

The process of engaging with critics can be understood through the lens of *dialogic communication theory*, which posits that effective communication arises from the interaction between differing viewpoints. According to Bakhtin (1981), dialogue is essential for understanding and co-creating meaning. This theory underlines the importance of listening, acknowledging, and responding to criticisms in a way that fosters mutual respect and understanding.

Moreover, *conflict resolution theory* emphasizes the need for constructive engagement in the face of opposition. Fisher and Ury (1981) suggest that focusing on interests rather than positions can lead to collaborative solutions. For LGBTQ activists, this means identifying shared values with critics, such as community safety or the welfare of youth, and using these commonalities as a foundation for dialogue.

Common Problems in Engagement

Despite the potential benefits, engaging with critics can present several challenges:

- **Emotional Responses:** Activists often face emotionally charged criticism that can provoke defensiveness. This reaction can derail productive conversations and escalate conflicts.

- **Misinformation:** Critics may spread misinformation about LGBTQ issues, leading to misunderstandings that require careful navigation to correct without alienating the audience.

- **Power Dynamics:** The inherent power imbalance in discussions, especially when critics hold significant influence (e.g., media figures, politicians), can complicate efforts to engage constructively.

- **Fear of Backlash:** Activists may worry that engaging with critics could result in further attacks or backlash, creating a reluctance to enter into dialogue.

Strategies for Constructive Engagement

To effectively engage with critics, LGBTQ activists can adopt several strategies:

1. **Active Listening:** Demonstrating genuine interest in the critic's perspective can defuse tension. Activists should practice reflective listening, summarizing the critic's points to show understanding before responding.

2. **Empathy and Validation:** Acknowledging the emotions and concerns of critics can foster a more respectful dialogue. For instance, when faced with a critic who expresses fear about changing societal norms, an activist might respond with, "I understand that change can be unsettling; let's explore what those changes mean for our community."

3. **Fact-Based Responses:** Countering misinformation with well-researched facts is crucial. Activists should prepare by gathering credible data and studies that support their positions. For example, when addressing claims that LGBTQ-inclusive policies harm children, citing peer-reviewed research that shows the benefits of inclusivity can be persuasive.

4. **Creating Safe Spaces for Dialogue:** Organizing forums or discussions where critics and supporters can engage in dialogue can demystify issues and reduce fear. By establishing ground rules for respectful communication, activists can facilitate more productive conversations.

5. **Highlighting Common Goals:** Finding shared values can bridge divides. Activists might point out that both sides desire a safe and supportive environment for all individuals, even if they disagree on methods.

6. **Follow-Up Engagement:** After initial discussions, following up with critics can demonstrate commitment to dialogue and understanding. Sending a thank-you message or sharing resources can keep lines of communication open.

Examples of Successful Engagement

Several prominent LGBTQ activists have navigated criticism effectively:

- **Laverne Cox:** As a transgender activist, Cox has faced significant backlash. In interviews, she often addresses critics by sharing her personal story, fostering empathy, and encouraging understanding through her lived experience.

- **Dan Savage:** The creator of the "It Gets Better" campaign has engaged with critics by addressing their concerns directly in his columns and podcasts. By using humor and facts, he disarms hostility and opens the door to dialogue.

- **The Trevor Project:** This organization has developed resources for educators and parents to address misconceptions about LGBTQ youth. By providing factual information and facilitating discussions, they have successfully engaged critics in educational contexts.

Conclusion

Constructively engaging with critics is an essential skill for LGBTQ activists. By employing strategies rooted in dialogue and conflict resolution theory, activists can transform adversarial interactions into opportunities for education and understanding. The ability to listen, empathize, and respond with facts can not only mitigate tensions but also foster a more inclusive environment for all. As the movement for LGBTQ rights continues to evolve, the importance of constructive engagement will only grow, paving the way for a more equitable future.

Bibliography

[1] Bakhtin, M. M. (1981). *The Dialogic Imagination: Four Essays*. University of Texas Press.

[2] Fisher, R., & Ury, W. (1981). *Getting to Yes: Negotiating Agreement Without Giving In*. Penguin Books.

Leveraging the Power of Media for Change

In the contemporary landscape of activism, media plays a pivotal role in shaping public perception and mobilizing support for LGBTQ rights. The strategic use of various media platforms allows activists to disseminate information, challenge stereotypes, and galvanize communities towards social change. This section explores the mechanisms through which Vex Aleron and other activists leverage media to amplify their message and foster a more inclusive society.

Understanding Media Influence

Media, in its myriad forms—traditional, digital, and social—serves as a conduit for information exchange. According to the *Agenda-Setting Theory*, media doesn't tell us what to think, but rather what to think about. This theory underscores the importance of media in shaping public discourse, particularly regarding marginalized communities. By prioritizing LGBTQ narratives, activists can influence societal attitudes and highlight issues that demand attention.

Strategies for Media Engagement

Activists like Vex Aleron employ several strategies to leverage media effectively:

- **Creating Compelling Narratives:** Personal stories are powerful tools for fostering empathy and understanding. By sharing authentic experiences, activists can humanize LGBTQ issues, making them relatable to a broader audience. For instance, Vex's journey of self-discovery and activism resonates with many, breaking down barriers of misunderstanding.

- **Utilizing Social Media Platforms:** The rise of platforms like Twitter, Instagram, and TikTok has revolutionized activism. These platforms allow for rapid dissemination of information and provide a space for marginalized voices. Vex capitalizes on these platforms to share updates on campaigns, promote events like the Kaevin Pride Parade, and engage in dialogue with followers.

- **Collaborating with Influencers and Allies:** Partnerships with public figures and influencers can significantly amplify messages. By aligning with those who have substantial followings, Vex expands the reach of LGBTQ advocacy. For example, collaborations with popular LGBTQ influencers can draw attention to specific campaigns, such as anti-discrimination legislation.

- **Creating Inclusive Media Content:** Vex advocates for the production of media that accurately represents LGBTQ lives. This includes supporting filmmakers, writers, and artists from the community to tell their stories. By promoting LGBTQ-inclusive content, activists can challenge prevailing stereotypes and foster a more nuanced understanding of diverse identities.

- **Engaging in Media Advocacy:** Activists must also hold media outlets accountable for their representation of LGBTQ issues. This includes critiquing biased coverage and advocating for fair representation. Vex participates in media panels and discussions to address misrepresentation and promote responsible journalism.

Challenges in Media Representation

Despite the opportunities media presents, several challenges persist:

- **Stereotyping and Misrepresentation:** LGBTQ individuals are often portrayed through a narrow lens, perpetuating harmful stereotypes. This misrepresentation can lead to societal stigma and discrimination. Activists must continuously confront these narratives and advocate for more accurate portrayals.

- **Censorship and Backlash:** In some regions, LGBTQ content faces censorship or backlash from conservative groups. This can hinder the

$$C = \sum_{i=1}^{n} P_i \qquad (25)$$

where C represents the coalition's collective power, and P_i represents the power of each individual group i. The more diverse and numerous the groups involved, the stronger the coalition becomes.

Challenges in Coalition Building

Despite the theoretical benefits, activists often encounter significant challenges when attempting to form coalitions. These challenges include:

- **Divergent Goals:** Different groups may have varying priorities, which can complicate the coalition's mission. For instance, while some LGBTQ organizations may prioritize marriage equality, others may focus on healthcare access or anti-discrimination laws.

- **Resource Allocation:** Disparities in funding and resources can create power imbalances within coalitions. Larger organizations may dominate discussions, sidelining smaller or grassroots groups that represent underrepresented communities.

- **Communication Barriers:** Effective communication is crucial for coalition success. Misunderstandings or lack of transparency can lead to mistrust and fragmentation.

- **Cultural Differences:** The LGBTQ community is incredibly diverse, encompassing various cultural backgrounds, beliefs, and experiences. Navigating these differences requires sensitivity and a willingness to learn from one another.

Successful Examples of Coalition Building

Successful coalitions provide powerful examples of how diverse groups can unite for a common cause. One notable instance is the collaboration between LGBTQ organizations and women's rights groups during the fight for reproductive rights. By joining forces, these groups were able to highlight the intersections of gender, sexuality, and reproductive justice, leading to more comprehensive policies that addressed the needs of all marginalized communities.

Another example is the formation of the "Black Lives Matter" movement, which has actively included LGBTQ voices and issues. This coalition has brought attention to the specific challenges faced by LGBTQ people of color, emphasizing the importance of intersectionality in activism. The movement's slogan, "Black Lives Matter," has been extended to include "Black LGBTQ Lives Matter," reinforcing the need for inclusivity within the broader fight for racial and sexual justice.

Strategies for Effective Coalition Building

To overcome the challenges of coalition building, activists can employ several strategies:

- **Establishing Common Goals:** It is essential to identify shared objectives that resonate with all coalition members. This common ground serves as a foundation for collaboration and unity.

- **Fostering Open Communication:** Regular meetings and open channels for dialogue can help build trust among coalition members. Utilizing technology, such as group chats and video conferencing, can facilitate ongoing communication.

- **Equitable Resource Sharing:** Developing a framework for resource allocation that ensures all voices are heard and valued can help mitigate power imbalances within the coalition.

- **Cultural Competency Training:** Providing training on cultural sensitivity and intersectionality can enhance understanding among coalition members and promote inclusivity.

Conclusion

Coalition building is a powerful tool in the pursuit of LGBTQ equality. By recognizing the complexities of diverse identities and experiences, activists can forge strong alliances that amplify their collective voice. The journey toward equality is not without its challenges, but through strategic collaboration and a commitment to inclusivity, coalitions can create lasting change in the fight for justice and equality for all.

The essence of coalition building can be summarized in the following equation, which reflects the potential for transformation when diverse groups unite:

$$C_{total} = C_1 + C_2 + C_3 + \ldots + C_n \qquad (26)$$

where C_{total} represents the total impact of the coalition, and C_i represents the contribution of each individual coalition member. Together, these contributions can lead to a more equitable society, where the rights of all individuals are respected and upheld.

Fostering Understanding and Empathy

In the realm of LGBTQ activism, fostering understanding and empathy is paramount. It serves as the bedrock upon which inclusive communities are built, bridging divides and dismantling stereotypes. This section explores the significance of empathy in activism, the challenges faced in fostering understanding, and practical strategies to promote these values.

The Importance of Empathy

Empathy, defined as the ability to understand and share the feelings of another, plays a crucial role in activism. According to [?], empathy allows individuals to transcend their own experiences and connect with the struggles of marginalized communities. It creates a sense of solidarity that is essential for collective action. In the context of LGBTQ rights, fostering empathy can lead to increased allyship and support from non-LGBTQ individuals, ultimately contributing to a more inclusive society.

Challenges in Fostering Understanding

Despite its importance, fostering understanding and empathy is fraught with challenges. One significant barrier is the prevalence of stereotypes and misinformation about LGBTQ individuals. Research by [?] indicates that negative stereotypes can lead to dehumanization, which in turn diminishes empathy. Furthermore, individuals from conservative backgrounds may harbor ingrained biases that hinder their ability to empathize with LGBTQ experiences.

Another challenge is the emotional toll that activism can take on LGBTQ individuals themselves. As [1] notes, the constant battle against discrimination can lead to fatigue and burnout, making it difficult for activists to engage in dialogues aimed at fostering understanding.

Strategies for Promoting Empathy

To effectively foster understanding and empathy, several strategies can be employed:

- **Storytelling:** Sharing personal narratives is a powerful tool in building empathy. According to [?], stories can evoke emotional responses that foster connection. Activists can organize events where LGBTQ individuals share their experiences, allowing others to see the humanity behind the labels.

- **Education and Workshops:** Conducting workshops aimed at educating non-LGBTQ individuals about LGBTQ issues can dismantle misconceptions. These workshops should include interactive elements that encourage participants to engage with LGBTQ narratives and experiences.

- **Collaborative Projects:** Engaging in community projects that require collaboration between LGBTQ and non-LGBTQ individuals can foster understanding. For example, joint initiatives in local schools or community centers can create opportunities for dialogue and relationship-building.

- **Utilizing Media:** Media representation plays a crucial role in shaping perceptions. By promoting inclusive media that accurately portrays LGBTQ lives, activists can challenge stereotypes and foster empathy. Documentaries, films, and social media campaigns can be effective in this regard.

Examples of Successful Empathy Initiatives

Several initiatives have successfully fostered understanding and empathy within communities. One notable example is the *It Gets Better* campaign, which started as a response to the bullying of LGBTQ youth. By sharing uplifting stories of LGBTQ individuals who have overcome adversity, the campaign has fostered empathy among viewers, encouraging allies to stand in support of LGBTQ rights.

Another example is the *Humans of New York* project, which features stories from diverse individuals, including members of the LGBTQ community. This platform humanizes the experiences of LGBTQ individuals, allowing audiences to connect on a personal level and fostering a greater sense of empathy.

Conclusion

Fostering understanding and empathy is essential for advancing LGBTQ rights and building inclusive communities. By recognizing the importance of empathy, addressing the challenges that hinder it, and employing effective strategies, activists can create environments where understanding flourishes. As we move forward, the commitment to fostering empathy will be a driving force in the ongoing fight for equality, ensuring that all voices are heard and valued.

Engaging with Religious and Conservative Groups

In the realm of LGBTQ activism, engaging with religious and conservative groups presents a unique set of challenges and opportunities. The historical context of LGBTQ rights often intersects with deeply held beliefs and values within these communities, making dialogue both essential and complex.

Understanding the Landscape

Religious institutions have traditionally held conservative views regarding sexual orientation and gender identity. This can lead to significant resistance against LGBTQ rights, often rooted in scriptural interpretations and cultural norms. For instance, many conservative Christian groups cite passages from religious texts as justification for their stance against same-sex relationships and gender diversity.

To navigate this landscape effectively, it is crucial for LGBTQ activists to understand the theological underpinnings of these beliefs. Engaging in interfaith dialogues can provide insights into how different denominations interpret scripture, allowing activists to identify common ground. For example, many progressive religious groups advocate for LGBTQ inclusion, demonstrating that not all faith-based perspectives are monolithic.

Building Bridges Through Dialogue

One effective strategy for engaging with conservative groups is to initiate respectful and open dialogues. This involves creating safe spaces where individuals from both sides can share their views without fear of judgment.

A notable example is the "Faith and Freedom Coalition," which works to promote understanding between LGBTQ activists and conservative Christians. By organizing community forums, they facilitate discussions that explore the intersection of faith and sexual identity.

$$\text{Dialogue} = \text{Respect} + \text{Understanding} + \text{Common Goals} \qquad (27)$$

This equation illustrates that successful dialogue requires a foundation of respect and understanding, with an emphasis on identifying common goals, such as community welfare and social justice.

Addressing Misconceptions

Misconceptions about LGBTQ identities often fuel animosity within religious and conservative circles. Activists can address these misconceptions through educational initiatives, providing accurate information about LGBTQ lives and experiences.

Workshops and seminars can be organized in collaboration with religious leaders who are sympathetic to LGBTQ issues. These events can serve as platforms for sharing personal stories, highlighting the diversity within the LGBTQ community, and dispelling myths that contribute to prejudice.

For instance, the "Religious Institute" has successfully partnered with LGBTQ organizations to create educational materials that clarify misconceptions regarding sexual orientation and gender identity.

Finding Common Ground

Despite differing viewpoints, there are often shared values that can be leveraged to foster collaboration. Issues such as family, love, and community welfare resonate across ideological lines.

By framing LGBTQ rights as a matter of human dignity and love, activists can appeal to the fundamental values held by many religious groups. For example, the "Love is Love" campaign emphasizes that love should not be restricted by gender, a message that can resonate with many faith-based communities.

$$\text{Common Ground} = \text{Shared Values} + \text{Mutual Respect} \qquad (28)$$

This equation signifies that the foundation for collaboration lies in recognizing shared values while maintaining mutual respect.

Navigating Resistance and Backlash

Engaging with religious and conservative groups is not without its challenges. Activists may face backlash, including accusations of undermining traditional values or engaging in "agenda-driven" politics.

It is essential to approach such resistance with resilience and a commitment to dialogue. For instance, during the campaign for marriage equality in the United States, many activists faced significant opposition from religious groups. However, through persistent engagement and community outreach, they were able to shift perceptions and garner support from unexpected allies.

Case Studies of Successful Engagement

Several case studies illustrate successful strategies for engaging with religious and conservative groups:

1. **The United Church of Christ**: This denomination has been at the forefront of advocating for LGBTQ rights within a religious context. By embracing LGBTQ members and affirming their rights, they have created a model for other religious groups to follow.

2. **The Interfaith Coalition for LGBTQ Justice**: This coalition brings together diverse faith leaders to advocate for LGBTQ rights. Their efforts demonstrate that faith communities can unite for social justice, regardless of differing theological views.

3. **The "Faith and LGBTQ" Initiative**: This initiative focuses on creating dialogue between LGBTQ activists and religious leaders. By sharing personal stories and emphasizing common values, they have successfully built alliances that promote understanding and acceptance.

Conclusion

Engaging with religious and conservative groups is a critical aspect of advancing LGBTQ rights. By fostering dialogue, addressing misconceptions, and finding common ground, activists can create a more inclusive environment for all individuals, regardless of their sexual orientation or gender identity. The journey toward equality requires patience, empathy, and a commitment to understanding diverse perspectives.

Ultimately, the goal is to create a society where love and acceptance triumph over prejudice and division, paving the way for a future where LGBTQ individuals can thrive in all aspects of life, including within their faith communities.

Uniting for a Common Goal

In the landscape of LGBTQ activism, the concept of unity transcends mere collaboration; it embodies a shared vision where diverse groups coalesce to advocate for equality and justice. This section explores the necessity of uniting for a common goal, the challenges faced, and the transformative power of solidarity in creating meaningful change.

The Importance of Unity

Unity among various organizations and individuals within the LGBTQ community is vital for amplifying voices and strengthening the movement. Theoretical frameworks such as *Collective Action Theory* suggest that individuals are more likely to engage in activism when they perceive that their efforts contribute to a larger, shared objective. This theory posits that coordinated efforts lead to increased resources, visibility, and impact, fostering an environment where marginalized voices are heard and valued.

Challenges to Unity

Despite the clear advantages of unity, LGBTQ activism often grapples with internal divisions based on race, gender identity, socioeconomic status, and differing political ideologies. For instance, the intersectionality of identities can create friction; LGBTQ people of color may feel sidelined in predominantly white LGBTQ spaces, while transgender individuals may encounter resistance from within the community itself. This fragmentation can hinder progress and dilute the message of equality.

To illustrate, during the planning of the first Kaevin Pride Parade, organizers faced challenges in representing the diverse spectrum of the LGBTQ community. Some factions argued that the focus should be solely on gay rights, while others emphasized the importance of including trans and non-binary voices. This discord highlighted the necessity of engaging in dialogue and fostering understanding among different groups to ensure that all perspectives are included in the fight for equality.

Building Coalitions

Successful activism requires building coalitions that encompass a wide range of stakeholders. This includes not only LGBTQ organizations but also allies from various sectors, such as education, healthcare, and business. By forming partnerships with non-LGBTQ organizations, activists can leverage additional resources and expertise to advocate for policy changes and social acceptance.

For example, the collaboration between LGBTQ activists and local businesses during the Kaevin Pride Parade not only provided financial support but also fostered a sense of community. Businesses displayed inclusive signage and hosted events leading up to the parade, thereby demonstrating their commitment to diversity. This partnership exemplified how uniting for a common goal can create a ripple effect, encouraging others to join the movement.

Engaging Religious and Conservative Groups

One of the most significant challenges in uniting for a common goal is engaging with religious and conservative groups that may hold opposing views on LGBTQ rights. However, fostering dialogue with these groups can lead to unexpected alliances. By emphasizing shared values, such as love, compassion, and community, activists can create spaces for understanding and collaboration.

For instance, an initiative in Kaevin brought together LGBTQ activists and moderate religious leaders to discuss common ground. This dialogue led to the formation of a coalition advocating for anti-discrimination legislation that included protections for LGBTQ individuals. Such efforts demonstrate that unity is not solely about agreement but about finding ways to work together toward shared objectives, even amidst differing beliefs.

The Role of Intersectionality

Uniting for a common goal also necessitates an intersectional approach, recognizing that individuals experience multiple forms of discrimination that must be addressed holistically. The concept of intersectionality, introduced by Kimberlé Crenshaw, serves as a critical framework for understanding how overlapping identities impact experiences of oppression and privilege.

In practice, this means that LGBTQ activists must prioritize inclusivity in their efforts. For instance, when organizing events, it is essential to consider accessibility for individuals with disabilities and to ensure that the needs of LGBTQ people of color are represented. By embracing intersectionality, the movement can build a stronger foundation for unity that reflects the diversity of the community.

The Transformative Power of Solidarity

Ultimately, uniting for a common goal transforms not only the movement but also the individuals involved. When people come together, they create a sense of belonging and empowerment that fuels further activism. The shared experiences of struggle and triumph can strengthen relationships and foster a culture of support within the community.

For example, during the Kaevin Pride Parade, participants from various backgrounds came together to celebrate their identities and advocate for their rights. The collective energy and enthusiasm demonstrated the power of solidarity, as individuals recognized that their voices, when united, could challenge the status quo and demand change.

Conclusion

In conclusion, uniting for a common goal is essential for the success of LGBTQ activism. While challenges persist, the potential for transformative change lies in the ability to build coalitions, engage diverse groups, and embrace an intersectional approach. By working together, activists can amplify their voices and create a more inclusive and equitable society for all. The journey toward unity may be complex, but the rewards—greater visibility, understanding, and acceptance—are invaluable in the ongoing fight for LGBTQ rights.

Activism in the Digital Age

Harnessing the Power of Social Media

In the contemporary landscape of activism, social media has emerged as a formidable tool for LGBTQ advocates, offering a platform for raising awareness, mobilizing support, and fostering community. This section explores the multifaceted ways in which social media can be harnessed to amplify LGBTQ voices and drive social change.

Theoretical Framework

The utilization of social media in activism can be understood through the lens of networked social movements theory. This theory posits that social movements are increasingly organized through networks rather than traditional hierarchical structures, allowing for rapid dissemination of information and mobilization of supporters. According to [?], the "networked public sphere" facilitates the emergence of new forms of activism that challenge established norms and create spaces for marginalized voices.

Opportunities Presented by Social Media

1. **Amplification of Voices** Social media platforms such as Twitter, Instagram, and Facebook allow individuals to share their stories and experiences with a global audience. This amplification is particularly vital for LGBTQ individuals who may feel isolated in their communities. For instance, the #LoveIsLove campaign gained traction on social media, showcasing the stories of same-sex couples and their fight for recognition and equality. This visibility not only fosters empathy but also encourages others to share their narratives, creating a ripple effect of awareness and solidarity.

2. **Mobilization and Organization**   Social media facilitates the rapid organization of events and protests. For example, the #BlackLivesMatter movement effectively utilized platforms like Twitter to mobilize supporters for protests and rallies, demonstrating how social media can serve as a catalyst for real-world action. LGBTQ activists have similarly leveraged these platforms to organize pride events, educational workshops, and advocacy campaigns, reaching a wider audience than traditional methods would allow.

3. **Building Community**   Social media provides a space for LGBTQ individuals to connect, share resources, and offer support. Online communities, such as LGBTQ-focused Facebook groups or Reddit forums, create safe spaces for individuals to discuss issues, seek advice, and find solidarity. The importance of these communities cannot be overstated, as they often serve as a lifeline for individuals facing discrimination or mental health challenges.

Challenges and Concerns

While social media offers numerous advantages, it also presents significant challenges for LGBTQ activists.

1. **Misinformation and Hate Speech**   The open nature of social media platforms can lead to the spread of misinformation and hate speech. For instance, during the debate over marriage equality, false information regarding the implications of same-sex marriage circulated widely, often fueled by organized opposition groups. Activists must navigate this landscape carefully, employing strategies to counter misinformation and promote accurate narratives.

2. **Cyberbullying and Harassment**   LGBTQ individuals often face targeted harassment online, which can deter participation in activism. According to a study by [?], a significant percentage of LGBTQ youth reported experiencing online harassment. This environment of hostility necessitates the development of robust strategies for protecting individuals and fostering safe online spaces.

3. **Digital Divide**   Not all LGBTQ individuals have equal access to social media platforms. The digital divide can exacerbate existing inequalities, leaving marginalized voices unheard. Activists must consider inclusivity in their digital strategies, ensuring that outreach efforts encompass those who may not have access to the internet or social media.

Best Practices for Effective Social Media Activism

To maximize the impact of social media in LGBTQ activism, several best practices should be adopted:

1. Authentic Storytelling   Engaging storytelling is crucial for connecting with audiences. Activists should prioritize authentic narratives that highlight personal experiences and foster empathy. For example, the "It Gets Better" project effectively utilized personal stories to provide hope and support to LGBTQ youth facing adversity.

2. Strategic Hashtag Use   Hashtags play a critical role in increasing visibility and organizing discussions. Activists should develop and promote specific hashtags that encapsulate their messages, making it easier for users to find and engage with relevant content. The hashtag #TransRightsAreHumanRights has been instrumental in raising awareness about transgender issues and mobilizing support.

3. Collaboration and Cross-Promotion   Collaborating with other activists and organizations can amplify messages and broaden reach. By cross-promoting content, LGBTQ activists can tap into established audiences and foster a sense of unity within the broader social justice movement.

Conclusion

Harnessing the power of social media is essential for the continued advancement of LGBTQ rights and visibility. While challenges persist, the opportunities presented by these platforms are immense. By employing strategic approaches and prioritizing inclusivity, LGBTQ activists can leverage social media to create lasting change, foster community, and challenge societal norms. As we move forward, it is crucial to remain vigilant against the challenges posed by misinformation and harassment, ensuring that the digital landscape remains a safe and empowering space for all.

Online Activism and its Impact

In the age of digital communication, online activism has emerged as a powerful tool for promoting LGBTQ rights and fostering community engagement. The internet provides a platform for marginalized voices, allowing activists to share their stories, mobilize support, and challenge oppressive systems. This section explores the multifaceted impact of online activism on the LGBTQ movement, highlighting both its advantages and challenges.

The Rise of Digital Platforms

The proliferation of social media platforms such as Twitter, Instagram, and Facebook has revolutionized the way activists communicate and organize. These platforms enable rapid dissemination of information, allowing campaigns to reach a global audience almost instantaneously. For instance, the hashtag #LoveIsLove became a rallying cry for marriage equality, uniting supporters across various demographics and geographical boundaries. This phenomenon aligns with the theory of *networked individualism*, where personal connections and social networks facilitate collective action [?].

Mobilization and Organization

Online activism fosters mobilization by lowering the barriers to participation. Individuals who may feel isolated in their communities can find solidarity and support through virtual spaces. Campaigns such as the #BlackLivesMatter movement have demonstrated the effectiveness of online organizing in addressing intersectional issues within the LGBTQ community, particularly concerning the experiences of LGBTQ people of color. The ability to create and share petitions, organize virtual events, and coordinate protests has empowered activists to take collective action with unprecedented speed.

Challenges of Online Activism

Despite its advantages, online activism is not without challenges. One significant issue is the phenomenon of *slacktivism*, where individuals engage in minimal effort actions, such as liking or sharing posts, without committing to deeper involvement. This raises questions about the effectiveness of online engagement in driving real-world change. A study by [?] suggests that while online activism can raise awareness, it often lacks the sustained commitment necessary for substantial policy change.

Moreover, the digital landscape is rife with misinformation and hate speech, which can undermine LGBTQ activism. Activists often face backlash from opponents who exploit online platforms to spread harmful narratives. This necessitates a strategic approach to counter misinformation, employing fact-checking and community education to combat falsehoods.

Case Studies of Impact

Several case studies illustrate the profound impact of online activism on LGBTQ rights:

- **The Pulse Nightclub Shooting:** Following the tragic shooting in 2016, social media became a vital space for mourning and organizing. Hashtags like #WeAreOrlando facilitated global solidarity and fundraising efforts for victims' families, showcasing the power of online communities in times of crisis.

- **Transgender Visibility:** The campaign for transgender rights has gained momentum through online platforms, with activists using social media to share personal narratives and advocate for policy changes. The #TransRightsAreHumanRights hashtag has helped to amplify transgender voices and highlight issues such as healthcare access and legal recognition.

- **Global LGBTQ Rights:** Online activism has transcended borders, allowing activists in countries with oppressive regimes to connect with international allies. The #FreeOurSisters campaign aimed at raising awareness about the plight of LGBTQ individuals in countries with anti-LGBTQ laws, illustrating how digital platforms can foster global solidarity.

The Future of Online Activism

As technology continues to evolve, so too will the strategies employed by LGBTQ activists. The rise of new platforms, such as TikTok, presents unique opportunities for creative expression and outreach. Engaging younger audiences through innovative content can further amplify LGBTQ voices and issues. However, activists must remain vigilant against emerging challenges, including algorithmic bias and the potential for digital surveillance.

In conclusion, online activism plays a crucial role in advancing LGBTQ rights and fostering community engagement. While it presents both opportunities and challenges, the ability to mobilize support, share stories, and connect with others remains a powerful asset in the ongoing fight for equality. As activists navigate the complexities of the digital landscape, their resilience and adaptability will be key to sustaining momentum and effecting change.

Addressing Cyberbullying and Online Hate

In the digital age, the rise of social media platforms has provided unprecedented opportunities for LGBTQ activism. However, this same digital landscape has also birthed a surge in cyberbullying and online hate, posing significant challenges for activists like Vex Aleron. Cyberbullying is defined as the use of digital technologies to harass, threaten, or humiliate individuals, often in a public forum. This phenomenon can have devastating effects on mental health, self-esteem, and overall well-being, particularly for marginalized groups such as the LGBTQ community.

The theoretical framework for understanding cyberbullying can be anchored in the Social Learning Theory, which posits that individuals learn behaviors through observation and imitation of others. In the context of online interactions, this means that individuals may engage in bullying behaviors after witnessing similar actions being normalized in their digital environments. This is exacerbated by the anonymity that the internet provides, allowing individuals to express hate without facing immediate consequences.

The Scope of the Problem

Cyberbullying against LGBTQ individuals often manifests in various forms, including derogatory comments, threats of violence, doxing (the act of publicly revealing private information), and the dissemination of false information. According to a study by the Cyberbullying Research Center, approximately 34% of LGBTQ youth have experienced cyberbullying, compared to 20% of their heterosexual peers. This disparity highlights the unique vulnerabilities faced by LGBTQ individuals in online spaces.

One notable case that exemplifies the severity of online hate is the backlash faced by Vex Aleron after organizing the first Kaevin Pride Parade. Following the announcement, Vex's social media accounts were inundated with hateful comments, including threats and slurs. This not only affected Vex personally but also created a chilling effect on other activists who feared similar repercussions for their involvement.

Strategies for Addressing Cyberbullying

To combat cyberbullying and online hate, Vex and other activists have implemented several strategies:
  1. **Education and Awareness Campaigns**: Raising awareness about the impact of cyberbullying is crucial. Educational campaigns that inform users about the consequences of their online behavior can foster a more respectful digital

culture. For instance, Vex collaborated with local schools to conduct workshops on digital citizenship and the importance of empathy in online interactions.

2. **Building Support Networks**: Creating safe spaces for LGBTQ individuals online can mitigate the effects of cyberbullying. Support networks, such as online forums and social media groups, provide platforms for individuals to share their experiences and seek help. Vex established a dedicated online support group for LGBTQ youth, offering resources and a safe haven for those affected by online hate.

3. **Reporting Mechanisms**: Encouraging users to report instances of cyberbullying is essential. Many social media platforms have built-in reporting features that allow users to flag abusive content. Vex actively promoted these tools within the community, emphasizing the importance of taking action against online hate.

4. **Legal Advocacy**: Advocating for stronger legal protections against cyberbullying is another critical aspect. Vex worked with local lawmakers to draft legislation that addresses online harassment and provides clearer avenues for victims to seek recourse. This includes proposing amendments to existing laws to include protections specifically for LGBTQ individuals.

5. **Mental Health Resources**: Addressing the mental health implications of cyberbullying is vital. Vex partnered with mental health organizations to provide resources and counseling for those affected by online hate. This initiative aimed to destigmatize seeking help and ensure that victims have access to the support they need.

Examples of Successful Interventions

One successful intervention was the "#StandWithVex" campaign, which aimed to counteract the negative narratives surrounding the Pride Parade. Activists and allies flooded social media with positive messages, stories of resilience, and expressions of solidarity. This campaign not only helped to drown out the hate but also empowered individuals to share their own experiences with cyberbullying, fostering a sense of community and support.

Another example involved a collaboration with tech companies to develop tools that detect and filter hate speech. By leveraging artificial intelligence, these tools can identify harmful content in real-time, allowing for quicker responses to cyberbullying incidents. Vex's involvement in this initiative underscored the importance of technology in combating online hate.

Conclusion

Addressing cyberbullying and online hate is an ongoing battle for LGBTQ activists like Vex Aleron. While the digital landscape offers a platform for advocacy and community building, it also presents significant risks that must be navigated carefully. Through education, support networks, legal advocacy, and technological innovations, activists can create safer online spaces for all individuals, ensuring that the fight for LGBTQ equality extends beyond the physical realm and into the digital world. As Vex often states, "Our voices are powerful, and together, we can silence the hate."

Utilizing Technology for Activism

In the modern landscape of activism, technology serves as a pivotal tool that empowers individuals and organizations to amplify their voices and mobilize supporters. The integration of digital platforms into LGBTQ activism has transformed traditional advocacy methods, enabling activists to reach a broader audience, engage in real-time discussions, and organize events with unprecedented efficiency. This section delves into the various ways technology is utilized in LGBTQ activism, the challenges faced, and notable examples of successful campaigns.

The Role of Social Media

Social media platforms such as Twitter, Instagram, Facebook, and TikTok have become essential venues for LGBTQ activists to share their messages and connect with allies. The immediacy of social media allows for rapid dissemination of information, which can be crucial during crises or moments of heightened visibility for LGBTQ issues. For instance, the hashtag #LoveIsLove emerged as a rallying cry during the push for marriage equality, uniting voices across the globe and creating a sense of solidarity among advocates.

Moreover, social media provides a space for marginalized voices within the LGBTQ community, such as transgender individuals and people of color, to share their experiences and advocate for their rights. The ability to create and share content, such as videos, memes, and infographics, enables activists to engage audiences in more relatable and impactful ways.

Online Campaigns and Fundraising

Technology has also revolutionized the way activists organize campaigns and raise funds. Crowdfunding platforms like GoFundMe and Kickstarter allow activists to gather financial support for specific initiatives, whether it's funding a local pride event or supporting legal battles for LGBTQ rights. For example, the `#TransRightsAreHumanRights` campaign successfully raised funds to support transgender individuals facing discrimination and violence, showcasing the power of digital fundraising.

Additionally, online petitions hosted on platforms like Change.org have proven effective in mobilizing public support for legislative changes. Activists can quickly gather signatures and demonstrate widespread backing for their causes, compelling lawmakers to take action. The petition for the repeal of the Defense of Marriage Act (DOMA) garnered over 300,000 signatures, illustrating the potential of online activism to influence policy decisions.

Challenges of Digital Activism

Despite the advantages of utilizing technology for activism, several challenges persist. One significant issue is the prevalence of online harassment and cyberbullying, particularly targeting LGBTQ individuals. Activists often face threats, hate speech, and doxxing, which can deter participation and silence voices. The impact of such harassment can lead to mental health challenges, emphasizing the need for supportive online communities and resources.

Moreover, the digital divide remains a barrier to equitable participation in online activism. Not all individuals have access to the internet or digital devices, disproportionately affecting marginalized groups within the LGBTQ community. This inequity can hinder the representation of diverse voices in digital spaces, limiting the effectiveness of online campaigns.

Utilizing Technology for Education and Awareness

Technology also plays a crucial role in educating the public about LGBTQ issues and fostering understanding. Online resources, such as websites, webinars, and virtual workshops, provide valuable information on topics ranging from sexual health to legal rights. Organizations like the Human Rights Campaign (HRC) and GLAAD have developed comprehensive online toolkits that equip activists and allies with the knowledge needed to advocate effectively.

Furthermore, the rise of podcasts and web series has created new avenues for storytelling within the LGBTQ community. These platforms allow individuals to share their personal narratives, fostering empathy and connection among listeners. For example, the podcast `Queery` explores the lives and experiences of LGBTQ individuals, promoting visibility and understanding through authentic storytelling.

Case Studies of Successful Digital Activism

Several notable campaigns exemplify the successful utilization of technology in LGBTQ activism. The `#BlackLivesMatter` movement, while primarily focused on racial justice, has intersectional ties to LGBTQ rights, particularly regarding the experiences of Black transgender individuals. The movement leveraged social media to raise awareness of systemic racism and police violence, fostering solidarity between racial and LGBTQ activists.

Another significant example is the `#MeToo` movement, which highlighted sexual harassment and assault across various industries. LGBTQ individuals played a vital role in this movement, sharing their stories and advocating for accountability. The viral nature of the campaign demonstrated the power of technology to create a global dialogue around issues of consent and safety, transcending traditional boundaries.

Conclusion

In conclusion, the utilization of technology for LGBTQ activism has reshaped the landscape of advocacy, providing new tools for engagement, education, and mobilization. While challenges such as online harassment and the digital divide persist, the potential for technology to amplify voices and foster community remains significant. As activists continue to navigate the evolving digital landscape, the lessons learned from past campaigns can inform future strategies, ensuring that the fight for LGBTQ equality remains vibrant and inclusive in the digital age.

Navigating Online Activist Spaces

In the digital age, online activist spaces have emerged as critical platforms for LGBTQ advocacy, allowing individuals to mobilize, share resources, and connect with like-minded allies across the globe. These spaces, however, are not without their complexities and challenges. Understanding the dynamics of online activism is essential for effective engagement and sustained impact.

Theoretical Framework

To navigate online activist spaces effectively, one must consider the theoretical frameworks that inform digital activism. The **Networked Publics** theory posits that social media platforms serve as new public spheres where marginalized voices can be amplified. According to [?], these digital environments facilitate both the dissemination of information and the formation of communities around shared identities and causes. This framework is particularly relevant for LGBTQ activists seeking to challenge societal norms and advocate for equality.

Challenges in Online Activism

Despite the advantages of online platforms, activists face several challenges:

- **Cyberbullying and Online Harassment:** LGBTQ activists often encounter targeted harassment and bullying in digital spaces. This can manifest as hate speech, doxxing, or coordinated attacks aimed at silencing voices of dissent. Research by [?] highlights the psychological toll that cyberbullying takes on individuals, particularly within marginalized communities.

- **Misinformation and Disinformation:** The rapid spread of false information can undermine activism efforts. For instance, during the COVID-19 pandemic, misinformation about LGBTQ individuals and health issues proliferated online, complicating public health messaging and advocacy efforts. Activists must develop strategies to combat misinformation, including fact-checking and promoting credible sources.

- **Digital Divide:** Access to technology and the internet is not universal. Many LGBTQ individuals, particularly those from marginalized backgrounds, may lack the resources to participate fully in online activism. This digital divide raises questions about inclusivity and representation in digital spaces.

Strategies for Effective Engagement

To navigate these challenges, LGBTQ activists can adopt several strategies:

1. **Building Safe Spaces:** Creating and maintaining online communities that prioritize safety and inclusivity is essential. This can involve implementing strict community guidelines, moderating discussions, and providing resources for mental health support. Platforms like Discord and private Facebook groups can serve as safe havens for LGBTQ activists.

2. **Leveraging Hashtags and Campaigns:** Activists can utilize hashtags to raise awareness and mobilize support for specific issues. For example, the hashtag #BlackLivesMatter has been instrumental in highlighting the intersection of

racial justice and LGBTQ rights. Engaging in trending campaigns can amplify voices and draw attention to critical issues.

3. **Collaborating Across Movements:** Intersectionality is key in online activism. Collaborating with other social justice movements can strengthen advocacy efforts. For instance, LGBTQ activists can work alongside racial justice advocates to address the unique challenges faced by LGBTQ people of color, fostering a more inclusive approach to activism.

Examples of Successful Online Activism

Several successful campaigns exemplify effective navigation of online activist spaces:

- **The Ice Cream for Everyone Campaign:** In response to anti-LGBTQ legislation, a group of activists launched a viral campaign encouraging ice cream shops to support LGBTQ rights. By using social media to share stories and images, they successfully pressured businesses to take a stand, resulting in widespread support and increased visibility for the LGBTQ community.

- **#TransRightsAreHumanRights:** This hashtag has mobilized thousands to advocate for transgender rights globally. The campaign has not only raised awareness but has also influenced policy changes in various regions, demonstrating the power of collective online action.

Conclusion

Navigating online activist spaces requires a nuanced understanding of the digital landscape, an awareness of the challenges faced by LGBTQ activists, and the implementation of effective strategies for engagement. By fostering safe communities, leveraging the power of social media, and collaborating across movements, LGBTQ activists can amplify their voices and drive meaningful change in the fight for equality. As the digital realm continues to evolve, so too must the approaches to activism, ensuring that all voices are heard and valued in the pursuit of justice.

Chapter 4

Intersectionality in LGBTQ Activism

Exploring Identity Beyond Sexual Orientation

In the realm of LGBTQ activism, it is paramount to recognize that sexual orientation is but one facet of a person's identity. As Vex Aleron navigates the complexities of advocacy, it becomes evident that a holistic understanding of identity encompasses a multitude of dimensions, including race, gender identity, socioeconomic status, and cultural background. This intersectional approach is essential for fostering inclusivity within the LGBTQ movement.

Theoretical Frameworks

To explore identity beyond sexual orientation, we can draw on intersectionality theory, which posits that various social identities intersect to create unique experiences of oppression and privilege. Coined by Kimberlé Crenshaw in the late 1980s, intersectionality emphasizes that individuals are not defined by a single identity but rather by the interplay of multiple identities. This framework allows activists like Vex to understand that the experiences of a queer person of color differ significantly from those of a white queer individual.

$$I = f(S, G, R, C, E) \tag{29}$$

Where:

- I = Identity
- S = Sexual Orientation
- G = Gender Identity

- R = Race/Ethnicity
- C = Class/Socioeconomic Status
- E = Other Identities (e.g., disability, age)

This equation illustrates that identity is a function of various factors, and understanding these intersections is crucial for effective advocacy.

Challenges Faced by Diverse Identities

Activists within the LGBTQ community often encounter challenges that are exacerbated by their intersecting identities. For instance, LGBTQ individuals of color face compounded discrimination that is both racially and sexually motivated. This dual marginalization can lead to unique barriers in accessing resources, support systems, and representation within both the LGBTQ community and broader society.

- **Racial Discrimination:** LGBTQ people of color may experience racism within LGBTQ spaces, which can alienate them from their community.
- **Cultural Expectations:** Many individuals face pressure from their cultural backgrounds to conform to heteronormative standards, leading to internal conflict and stress.
- **Economic Barriers:** Socioeconomic disparities can limit access to healthcare, legal support, and safe spaces, further marginalizing these individuals.

Examples of Intersectional Advocacy

Vex Aleron's journey highlights the importance of intersectional activism. For instance, during the organization of the first Kaevin Pride Parade, Vex ensured that the event was inclusive of various identities by actively collaborating with local organizations that represent LGBTQ people of color, transgender individuals, and those with disabilities. This collaboration not only broadened the scope of the event but also fostered a sense of belonging among attendees.

> "We are not just fighting for our right to love; we are fighting for our right to exist in all our complexities," Vex proclaimed during a community meeting. This statement encapsulates the essence of intersectional activism, emphasizing that the fight for LGBTQ rights must also address the unique challenges faced by diverse identities.

The Role of Education and Awareness

To foster a more inclusive LGBTQ movement, education plays a pivotal role. Activists must engage in continuous learning about the various identities within the community. Workshops, seminars, and community discussions can serve as platforms for sharing knowledge and experiences. For example, Vex initiated a series of workshops titled "Beyond the Rainbow: Understanding Intersectionality in LGBTQ Activism," which aimed to educate allies and community members about the importance of inclusivity.

Conclusion

Exploring identity beyond sexual orientation is not merely an academic exercise; it is a necessary approach for creating a more equitable and inclusive LGBTQ movement. By embracing intersectionality, activists like Vex Aleron can challenge the status quo and ensure that all voices are heard and represented. The journey toward equality is multifaceted, and recognizing the complexities of identity is a crucial step in the fight for justice and acceptance for all individuals, regardless of their sexual orientation or intersecting identities.

In the words of Vex, "Our strength lies in our diversity, and our unity will pave the way for a brighter future for all."

Addressing the Challenges of LGBTQ People of Color

The intersection of race and sexual orientation presents unique challenges for LGBTQ individuals of color, often resulting in a compounded experience of discrimination and marginalization. This section aims to explore these challenges, drawing on relevant theories and examples to illustrate the complexities faced by this demographic.

Theoretical Frameworks

To understand the challenges faced by LGBTQ people of color, we can apply the concept of *intersectionality*, coined by Kimberlé Crenshaw in 1989. Intersectionality posits that individuals experience overlapping identities that can lead to unique forms of oppression. For LGBTQ people of color, this means that their experiences cannot be understood solely through the lens of sexual orientation or race but must be viewed as a confluence of both identities.

$$\text{Oppression}_{\text{total}} = f(\text{Race, Sexual Orientation, Socioeconomic Status, Gender Identity}) \tag{30}$$

This equation suggests that the totality of oppression experienced by an individual is a function of multiple intersecting identities. For instance, a Black transgender woman may face discrimination not only for her race but also for her gender identity and sexual orientation, which can lead to heightened vulnerability.

Socioeconomic Challenges

LGBTQ people of color often face socioeconomic disadvantages that further exacerbate their struggles. According to a report by the Williams Institute, LGBTQ individuals of color are more likely to experience poverty compared to their white counterparts. Factors contributing to this disparity include systemic racism, lack of access to quality education, and employment discrimination.

$$\text{Poverty Rate}_{\text{LGBTQ POC}} > \text{Poverty Rate}_{\text{LGBTQ White}} \tag{31}$$

This inequality is evident in employment statistics, where LGBTQ people of color often find themselves in lower-paying jobs and have less access to career advancement opportunities. For example, a study by the Human Rights Campaign found that LGBTQ people of color reported higher rates of workplace discrimination, which can lead to job instability and financial insecurity.

Health Disparities

Health disparities are another significant challenge faced by LGBTQ people of color. The National LGBTQ Task Force highlights that this group experiences higher rates of mental health issues, substance abuse, and chronic illnesses compared to white LGBTQ individuals. These disparities can be attributed to multiple factors, including stigma, lack of culturally competent healthcare providers, and inadequate access to healthcare services.

$$\text{Health Disparity} = \frac{\text{Health Issues}_{\text{LGBTQ POC}}}{\text{Access to Healthcare}_{\text{LGBTQ POC}}} \tag{32}$$

This equation indicates that the health disparities faced by LGBTQ people of color can be compounded by their limited access to healthcare resources. For instance, many LGBTQ people of color report avoiding medical care due to fear of discrimination, leading to untreated health issues.

Community and Identity Struggles

LGBTQ people of color often navigate complex identities that can lead to feelings of isolation within both the LGBTQ community and their racial or ethnic communities. Many individuals report feeling marginalized within LGBTQ spaces, where issues related to race may be overlooked or dismissed. Conversely, they may also experience rejection from their racial or ethnic communities due to their sexual orientation.

This dual marginalization can lead to a sense of alienation, as illustrated by the experiences of individuals like Marsha P. Johnson, a Black transgender activist who played a pivotal role in the Stonewall uprising. Despite her contributions to the LGBTQ movement, Johnson faced discrimination within both the LGBTQ community and the broader society, highlighting the need for greater inclusivity and recognition of the contributions of LGBTQ people of color.

Advocacy and Representation

Addressing the challenges faced by LGBTQ people of color requires intentional advocacy and representation. Organizations such as the National Black Justice Coalition (NBJC) and the Transgender Law Center (TLC) work to amplify the voices of LGBTQ people of color, advocating for policies that address their unique needs. These organizations focus on issues such as criminal justice reform, healthcare access, and economic empowerment, recognizing that intersectional advocacy is essential for achieving true equality.

Moreover, representation in media and politics plays a crucial role in shaping societal perceptions and fostering acceptance. The visibility of LGBTQ people of color in mainstream media can challenge stereotypes and promote understanding. For example, shows like *Pose* and films like *Moonlight* have brought attention to the experiences of LGBTQ people of color, highlighting their struggles and triumphs.

Conclusion

In conclusion, addressing the challenges of LGBTQ people of color requires a multifaceted approach that acknowledges the intersectionality of their identities. By understanding the unique experiences of this community, advocates can work towards creating more inclusive spaces and policies that address their specific needs. The fight for LGBTQ equality must include the voices of those who face compounded discrimination, ensuring that all individuals can live authentically and without fear of marginalization.

Centering Transgender and Non-Binary Voices

In the landscape of LGBTQ activism, centering transgender and non-binary voices is not merely an act of inclusion; it is a fundamental necessity for a truly equitable movement. Transgender and non-binary individuals face unique challenges that are often exacerbated by societal norms and systemic discrimination. This section explores the importance of amplifying these voices, the specific issues they encounter, and strategies for fostering a more inclusive activist environment.

Theoretical Framework

To understand the significance of centering transgender and non-binary voices, we can draw upon intersectionality theory, as proposed by Kimberlé Crenshaw. Intersectionality posits that individuals experience oppression in varying degrees based on multiple identities, including gender, race, and class. For transgender and non-binary individuals, their experiences are not monolithic; they intersect with various social categories that shape their realities. Thus, activism that fails to acknowledge these intersections risks perpetuating existing inequalities within the LGBTQ movement.

Challenges Faced by Transgender and Non-Binary Individuals

Transgender and non-binary individuals encounter a myriad of challenges that necessitate their voices being at the forefront of LGBTQ activism:

- **Healthcare Disparities:** Access to gender-affirming healthcare is a critical issue. Many transgender individuals face barriers such as discrimination from healthcare providers, lack of insurance coverage for necessary procedures, and a general lack of understanding about transgender health issues. According to the 2015 U.S. Transgender Survey, 33% of respondents reported having at least one negative experience with a healthcare provider related to their transgender status.

- **Violence and Discrimination:** Transgender individuals, especially transgender women of color, are disproportionately affected by violence. The Human Rights Campaign reports that in recent years, the number of violent deaths of transgender individuals has risen alarmingly, highlighting the urgent need for advocacy and protective legislation.

- **Mental Health Challenges:** The stigma associated with being transgender or non-binary can lead to significant mental health challenges. Studies show that transgender individuals experience higher rates of depression, anxiety, and suicidal ideation compared to their cisgender counterparts. A supportive community and representation can play a crucial role in mitigating these issues.

- **Legal Barriers:** Many transgender individuals face challenges in changing their legal documents to reflect their gender identity. This can lead to complications in various aspects of life, including employment, housing, and accessing services. The lack of comprehensive anti-discrimination laws further exacerbates these issues.

Examples of Centering Transgender and Non-Binary Voices

Several organizations and movements have successfully centered transgender and non-binary voices in their activism:

- **Transgender Law Center:** This organization focuses on changing law and policy to advance the rights of transgender and gender non-conforming people. They work on issues such as healthcare access, legal recognition, and combating discrimination.

- **Trans Lifeline:** A peer support service run by and for transgender people, Trans Lifeline provides critical resources for individuals in crisis. Their work emphasizes the importance of community support and the need for transgender voices in mental health advocacy.

- **#TransIsBeautiful Campaign:** Initiated by Geena Rocero, this campaign aims to celebrate transgender beauty and existence. By uplifting transgender stories and experiences, it creates a positive narrative that counters mainstream media representations often steeped in negativity.

- **The Gender Spectrum:** This organization focuses on creating a more inclusive world for people of all genders. Their programs and resources emphasize the importance of understanding and respecting non-binary identities, fostering environments where individuals can express their gender authentically.

Strategies for Inclusion

To ensure that transgender and non-binary voices are centered in LGBTQ activism, several strategies can be employed:

- **Active Listening:** Activists must prioritize listening to the experiences and needs of transgender and non-binary individuals. This includes creating spaces where their voices can be heard without interruption or invalidation.

- **Education and Awareness:** Providing education on transgender and non-binary issues within activist circles can foster understanding and empathy. Workshops, panel discussions, and resource sharing can help dismantle misconceptions and biases.

- **Policy Advocacy:** Advocating for policies that specifically address the needs of transgender and non-binary individuals is crucial. This includes supporting legislation that protects against discrimination and ensures access to healthcare.

- **Representation in Leadership:** Ensuring that transgender and non-binary individuals hold leadership positions within LGBTQ organizations is vital. Representation matters, as it brings diverse perspectives and experiences to the decision-making process.

- **Intersectional Collaboration:** Collaborating with other marginalized groups can strengthen the movement. By recognizing the interconnectedness of various struggles, activists can build solidarity and amplify each other's voices.

Conclusion

Centering transgender and non-binary voices is essential for a comprehensive and effective LGBTQ rights movement. By acknowledging the unique challenges faced by these individuals and actively working to amplify their voices, the movement can foster a more inclusive and equitable society. As we continue to strive for equality, it is imperative that we listen, learn, and act in solidarity with our transgender and non-binary siblings, ensuring that their experiences and needs are at the heart of our activism.

Including LGBTQ Individuals with Disabilities

The intersection of LGBTQ identities and disabilities represents a critical yet often overlooked aspect of the broader equality movement. Individuals who identify as both LGBTQ and disabled face unique challenges that can compound discrimination and marginalization. The need for inclusive activism that addresses these challenges is paramount, as it ensures that all voices within the community are heard and represented.

Understanding Intersectionality

Intersectionality, a term coined by legal scholar Kimberlé Crenshaw, provides a framework for understanding how various forms of social stratification, such as race, gender, sexual orientation, and disability, intersect to create unique experiences of oppression and privilege. For LGBTQ individuals with disabilities, this means that their experiences cannot be fully understood by examining their sexual orientation or disability in isolation. Instead, it is essential to consider how these identities interact to shape their realities.

The theory of intersectionality posits that individuals experience discrimination in multifaceted ways, resulting in compounded disadvantages. For example, a queer person with a physical disability may face barriers not only in accessing LGBTQ spaces but also in receiving appropriate disability accommodations. This can lead to feelings of isolation and exclusion from both the LGBTQ community and disability advocacy groups.

Barriers to Inclusion

Several barriers hinder the inclusion of LGBTQ individuals with disabilities within the broader LGBTQ movement:

1. **Physical Accessibility**: Many LGBTQ events and spaces are not physically accessible to individuals with disabilities. This includes inadequate wheelchair access, lack of sensory accommodations, and environments that do not consider the diverse needs of attendees. For instance, a pride parade may route through areas that are difficult for individuals with mobility impairments to navigate, effectively excluding them from participation.

2. **Representation in Leadership**: Leadership within LGBTQ organizations often lacks representation from disabled individuals. This absence can lead to policies and initiatives that do not consider the needs and perspectives of LGBTQ individuals with disabilities. For example, decisions regarding event planning, outreach, and advocacy may overlook critical accessibility considerations, perpetuating exclusion.

3. **Stereotypes and Stigma**: LGBTQ individuals with disabilities may face unique stereotypes that further marginalize them. For instance, the belief that disabled individuals are asexual or incapable of romantic relationships can lead to their exclusion from discussions around LGBTQ love and relationships. This

stigma not only affects their self-image but also impacts their ability to form connections within the community.

4. **Mental Health Challenges**: The intersection of LGBTQ identities and disabilities can lead to increased mental health challenges, including anxiety and depression. The societal stigma associated with both identities can exacerbate feelings of isolation. Activists must recognize the importance of mental health support tailored to the unique experiences of LGBTQ individuals with disabilities.

Examples of Inclusive Practices

To foster inclusion, LGBTQ organizations and movements can adopt several best practices:

1. **Accessibility Audits**: Conducting thorough accessibility audits of events and spaces can help identify barriers and ensure that LGBTQ individuals with disabilities can participate fully. This includes evaluating physical access, sensory accommodations, and the availability of support services.

2. **Diverse Representation**: Actively seeking to include LGBTQ individuals with disabilities in leadership roles within organizations can help ensure that their perspectives are considered in decision-making processes. This can involve mentorship programs, outreach efforts, and creating spaces for disabled voices to be amplified.

3. **Awareness Campaigns**: Developing awareness campaigns that highlight the experiences of LGBTQ individuals with disabilities can help challenge stereotypes and promote understanding within the broader community. Storytelling initiatives, workshops, and educational materials can serve to inform others about the unique challenges faced by this intersectional group.

4. **Collaborative Advocacy**: Building coalitions between LGBTQ organizations and disability advocacy groups can create a more unified front for promoting equality. By working together, these groups can address shared goals, such as accessible healthcare, anti-discrimination policies, and public awareness campaigns.

Conclusion

Including LGBTQ individuals with disabilities in the fight for equality is not just a matter of fairness; it is essential for the movement's integrity and effectiveness. By recognizing and addressing the unique challenges faced by this community, activists can create a more inclusive and equitable society. The fight for LGBTQ rights must encompass all identities, ensuring that no one is left behind. Only by embracing diversity within the LGBTQ community can we hope to achieve true equality for all.

$$\text{Inclusion} = \text{Accessibility} + \text{Representation} + \text{Awareness} + \text{Collaboration} \quad (33)$$

Embracing Diversity within the LGBTQ Community

The LGBTQ community is not a monolith; it is a vibrant tapestry woven from diverse identities, experiences, and cultures. Embracing this diversity is crucial for the movement's strength and effectiveness. In this section, we will explore the importance of inclusivity, the challenges faced by various subgroups, and the transformative power of intersectional activism.

Understanding Intersectionality

Intersectionality, a term coined by Kimberlé Crenshaw, refers to the interconnected nature of social categorizations such as race, class, and gender, which create overlapping systems of discrimination or disadvantage. In the context of LGBTQ activism, intersectionality highlights how individuals experience oppression differently based on their multiple identities. For instance, a queer person of color may face unique challenges that differ from those encountered by a white gay man or a cisgender lesbian.

$$D = f(I_1, I_2, I_3, \ldots, I_n) \quad (34)$$

Where D represents the diversity of experiences, and I_n denotes the various identities individuals hold, such as race, gender identity, sexual orientation, socioeconomic status, and ability.

The Challenges of LGBTQ People of Color

LGBTQ people of color often face compounded discrimination. According to the 2015 U.S. Transgender Survey, 47% of Black transgender individuals reported being sexually assaulted at some point in their lives, compared to 10% of white transgender individuals. This disparity highlights a critical need for activism that addresses both racial and sexual identity issues.

$$R = \frac{S}{E} \quad (35)$$

Where R is the rate of discrimination, S represents the severity of the discrimination faced, and E denotes the existing support systems available. The lower the E, the higher the R, indicating a dire need for enhanced support networks.

Centering Transgender and Non-Binary Voices

Transgender and non-binary individuals often find themselves marginalized within the broader LGBTQ community. Their voices must be amplified in discussions about rights, representation, and resources. Activists must prioritize the inclusion of transgender and non-binary perspectives in policy-making and community organizing.

For example, initiatives like the Transgender Day of Visibility and the Transgender Day of Remembrance serve as platforms to honor the lives and contributions of transgender individuals while also raising awareness of the violence they face.

Including LGBTQ Individuals with Disabilities

The intersection of disability and LGBTQ identity presents unique challenges. Many LGBTQ individuals with disabilities experience double marginalization. The Americans with Disabilities Act (ADA) has made strides in ensuring rights for disabled individuals, yet the intersectional needs of LGBTQ individuals with disabilities are often overlooked.

$$C = \sum_{i=1}^{n}(D_i + L_i) \qquad (36)$$

Where C represents the comprehensive care needed, D_i denotes the disability-related needs, and L_i signifies the LGBTQ-specific needs. This equation illustrates the necessity for a holistic approach to advocacy that addresses both aspects.

Embracing Diversity through Representation

Embracing diversity within the LGBTQ community also means ensuring representation in leadership roles. Representation matters; it shapes policies and practices that affect marginalized communities. Organizations that prioritize diversity in their leadership are more likely to create inclusive environments that reflect the needs of all community members.

For instance, the Human Rights Campaign (HRC) has made significant efforts to include diverse voices in its leadership, resulting in more effective advocacy for issues affecting LGBTQ people of color, transgender individuals, and those with disabilities.

The Transformative Power of Intersectional Activism

Intersectional activism recognizes that the fight for LGBTQ rights is inherently linked to broader social justice movements. Issues such as racial equality, economic justice, and disability rights intersect with LGBTQ advocacy. By embracing diversity, activists can build coalitions that amplify their collective voices and create systemic change.

One notable example is the collaboration between LGBTQ organizations and Black Lives Matter, which seeks to address both racial injustice and LGBTQ rights. Such partnerships exemplify how embracing diversity can lead to a more robust and inclusive movement.

Conclusion

Embracing diversity within the LGBTQ community is not merely an ethical obligation; it is a strategic necessity. By recognizing and addressing the unique challenges faced by various subgroups, the movement can foster a more inclusive environment that empowers all its members. Intersectional activism serves as a powerful tool for dismantling systemic oppression and building a future where everyone can live authentically and freely. As we continue to advocate for LGBTQ rights, let us commit to embracing the full spectrum of identities within our community, ensuring that no one is left behind in the fight for equality.

Legacy and Future

Celebrating Achievements and Milestones

In the journey toward LGBTQ equality, celebrating achievements and milestones serves as a crucial mechanism for motivation, validation, and community building. Each success, whether big or small, acts as a beacon of hope and a reminder of the progress made amidst the struggles. This section delves into the significance of these celebrations, highlighting key achievements within the LGBTQ rights movement, and addressing the theory behind the importance of recognition in activism.

The Significance of Celebrating Achievements

Celebrating achievements in the LGBTQ rights movement is not merely an act of recognition; it is an essential component of sustaining momentum. According to social movement theory, recognition of accomplishments can bolster group identity and solidarity, fostering a sense of belonging among activists. This sense of community is vital for maintaining engagement and enthusiasm, particularly in the face of ongoing challenges.

$$\text{Community Engagement} = f(\text{Recognition, Solidarity, Shared Goals}) \qquad (37)$$

Where: - Community Engagement refers to the active participation and involvement of individuals in the movement. - Recognition is the acknowledgment of achievements. - Solidarity reflects the unity among members of the community. - Shared Goals represent the common objectives that drive the movement forward.

Key Milestones in LGBTQ Rights

The LGBTQ rights movement has witnessed numerous milestones that deserve celebration. One of the most significant achievements was the legalization of same-sex marriage in various countries. For instance, in 2015, the United States Supreme Court ruled in *Obergefell v. Hodges*, affirming the right to marry for same-sex couples. This landmark decision not only represented a legal victory but also symbolized societal acceptance and the breaking down of long-standing prejudices.

Similarly, the repeal of "Don't Ask, Don't Tell" in 2011 marked a pivotal moment for LGBTQ individuals in the military, allowing them to serve openly without fear of discrimination. Celebrating these milestones through parades, public speeches, and community gatherings reinforces their significance and inspires future generations.

The Role of Pride Events

Pride events play a central role in celebrating LGBTQ achievements. These gatherings not only commemorate the progress made but also serve as a platform for raising awareness about ongoing issues. For instance, the first Pride Parade in 1970 commemorated the Stonewall riots of 1969, which were a catalyst for the modern LGBTQ rights movement. Today, Pride events around the world celebrate diversity, inclusion, and the resilience of the community.

Pride Event Impact = Awareness+Community Engagement+Cultural Expression
(38)

Where: - Pride Event Impact quantifies the overall effect of Pride events on society. - Awareness refers to the increased understanding of LGBTQ issues. - Community Engagement reflects participation in the events. - Cultural Expression encompasses the artistic and creative manifestations of LGBTQ identities.

Recognizing Unsung Heroes

While large-scale achievements receive significant attention, it is equally important to recognize the unsung heroes within the LGBTQ community. Activists who work tirelessly behind the scenes, often without recognition, play a vital role in driving change. This includes grassroots organizers, educators, and mental health advocates who provide support and resources to LGBTQ individuals. Celebrating their contributions fosters a culture of appreciation and encourages others to join the movement.

Challenges in Recognition

Despite the importance of celebrating achievements, challenges persist. The LGBTQ community often faces backlash and erasure of its history. For example, the contributions of LGBTQ people of color are frequently overlooked in mainstream narratives. Addressing these disparities is crucial to ensure that all voices are heard and celebrated.

Moreover, the commercialization of Pride events can dilute their original purpose. As corporations seek to capitalize on LGBTQ visibility, there is a risk that the focus shifts away from activism toward profit. It is essential for activists to remain vigilant and ensure that celebrations serve as a platform for advocacy and not merely as marketing opportunities.

Conclusion

In conclusion, celebrating achievements and milestones within the LGBTQ rights movement is vital for sustaining momentum and fostering community engagement. Recognizing both major victories and the contributions of individuals at all levels strengthens the movement and inspires future generations. As we continue to navigate the complexities of advocacy, it is imperative to honor our past, celebrate our present, and pave the way for a future where equality is not just an aspiration but a reality for all.

Inspiring the Next Generation of Activists

In the ever-evolving landscape of LGBTQ activism, the importance of inspiring the next generation cannot be overstated. As Vex Aleron navigated the tumultuous waters of advocacy in Kaevin, they recognized that the legacy of activism is not merely about the battles fought and won, but also about planting the seeds of courage, resilience, and determination in the hearts of young activists. This section delves into the strategies, theories, and examples that illustrate the crucial role of mentorship, education, and community engagement in nurturing the leaders of tomorrow.

Theoretical Framework

To understand the dynamics of inspiring future activists, we can draw on the Social Learning Theory proposed by Albert Bandura. This theory posits that individuals learn behaviors through observation, imitation, and modeling. In the context of LGBTQ activism, young people are more likely to engage in advocacy when they see role models—like Vex—who embody the values of resilience, courage, and inclusivity. Thus, creating opportunities for youth to interact with established activists allows for the transfer of knowledge and skills necessary for effective advocacy.

Mentorship Programs

One of the most effective ways to inspire the next generation is through structured mentorship programs. By pairing young activists with seasoned leaders, organizations can foster an environment of growth and learning. For instance, the Kaevin Youth Alliance established a mentorship initiative that connects high school students with local LGBTQ leaders. This program not only provides guidance but also creates a safe space for youth to explore their identities and develop their advocacy skills.

$$M = \sum_{i=1}^{n} \frac{E_i}{R_i} \qquad (39)$$

Where M represents the overall effectiveness of the mentorship program, E_i is the engagement level of each mentee, and R_i is the resources provided to each mentorship pair. This equation highlights the importance of both engagement and resources in determining the success of mentorship initiatives.

Educational Workshops

In addition to mentorship, educational workshops play a vital role in equipping young activists with the tools they need to succeed. Workshops focused on topics such as public speaking, community organizing, and digital activism empower youth to take action. For example, Vex organized a series of workshops titled "Activism 101," which covered the history of LGBTQ rights, effective protest strategies, and the importance of intersectionality in activism. These workshops not only educated participants but also instilled a sense of agency and purpose.

Community Engagement

Engaging the community is another essential aspect of inspiring future activists. Vex understood that activism is most effective when it is rooted in the community's needs and experiences. By involving young people in community service projects, advocacy campaigns, and local events, they foster a sense of belonging and responsibility. For instance, the annual Kaevin Pride Festival became a platform for youth to showcase their talents, share their stories, and connect with like-minded individuals.

Through community engagement, young activists learn the importance of collaboration and solidarity. The equation below illustrates the relationship between community engagement and the growth of activism:

$$A = C \times E \tag{40}$$

Where A represents the level of activism, C is the community engagement factor, and E is the empowerment level of the individuals involved. This relationship emphasizes that as community engagement increases, so does the overall activism within that community.

Celebrating Diversity

Inspiring the next generation of activists also involves celebrating the diversity within the LGBTQ community. Vex championed the idea that every voice matters, and that intersectionality is crucial in the fight for equality. By highlighting the stories of LGBTQ individuals from various backgrounds, including people of color, transgender individuals, and those with disabilities, young activists are encouraged to embrace their unique identities and advocate for a more inclusive movement.

$$D = \frac{V}{T} \tag{41}$$

Where D represents the diversity of the movement, V is the variety of voices included, and T is the total number of activists involved. This equation illustrates that greater diversity leads to a richer and more effective advocacy effort.

Conclusion

In conclusion, inspiring the next generation of LGBTQ activists is a multifaceted endeavor that requires mentorship, education, community engagement, and a commitment to celebrating diversity. As Vex Aleron demonstrated through their work in Kaevin, the future of activism lies in empowering young people to find their voices, embrace their identities, and take action for equality. By investing in the leaders of tomorrow, we ensure that the fight for LGBTQ rights continues to thrive, evolve, and inspire future generations to come.

Passing the Torch to Future Leaders

In the realm of LGBTQ activism, the concept of "passing the torch" is not merely a symbolic gesture; it is a crucial mechanism for ensuring the sustainability and evolution of the movement. As Vex Aleron reflects on their journey, the importance of mentorship and the transfer of knowledge to emerging leaders becomes evident. This section delves into the significance of fostering new talent within the LGBTQ community, the challenges faced in this transition, and the transformative potential that future leaders hold.

The Importance of Mentorship

Mentorship is a foundational element in the development of future leaders. According to [?], mentorship involves a relationship where a more experienced individual provides guidance, support, and encouragement to a less experienced counterpart. In the context of LGBTQ activism, mentors can provide invaluable insights into navigating the complexities of advocacy, policy-making, and community engagement. Vex Aleron, having faced numerous challenges throughout their career, understands the necessity of sharing experiences to empower the next generation.

For instance, Vex initiated a mentorship program within the Student Alliance for Equality, aimed at pairing seasoned activists with young, aspiring leaders. This program not only facilitated skill development but also fostered a sense of belonging among participants, which is vital in a community often marginalized by societal norms. The success of this initiative highlights the potential for mentorship to create a ripple effect, wherein knowledge and passion for activism are transmitted across generations.

Challenges in Transitioning Leadership

Despite the clear benefits of mentorship, several challenges can impede the effective passing of the torch. One significant issue is the generational divide within the LGBTQ community. As noted by [?], differing perspectives on activism can create friction between older and younger generations. Older activists may prioritize traditional forms of advocacy, while younger leaders often embrace digital platforms and social media as primary tools for engagement.

Moreover, the intersectionality of identities within the LGBTQ spectrum complicates mentorship dynamics. As Vex encountered, not all leaders share the same experiences or backgrounds, which can lead to disparities in the resources and support available to emerging activists. Addressing these challenges requires a commitment to inclusivity and a willingness to adapt mentorship approaches to cater to diverse needs.

Empowering Future Leaders through Education

Education plays a pivotal role in preparing future leaders to take on the mantle of activism. Vex Aleron championed the integration of LGBTQ studies into school curricula, emphasizing the importance of historical context and contemporary issues facing the community. By equipping young activists with knowledge about the struggles and triumphs of those who came before them, they are better prepared to navigate the complexities of the current landscape.

In addition, Vex organized workshops focused on skill-building in areas such as public speaking, advocacy strategies, and coalition-building. These workshops not only imparted practical skills but also instilled confidence in participants, enabling them to step into leadership roles with assurance. The impact of such educational initiatives can be profound, as evidenced by the emergence of several young activists who have since taken prominent roles within the movement.

The Transformative Potential of New Leaders

The future of LGBTQ activism lies in the hands of those who are willing to challenge the status quo and innovate. Emerging leaders bring fresh perspectives and ideas that can invigorate the movement. For example, the recent rise of digital activism has transformed how campaigns are organized and executed. Young activists have harnessed social media platforms to amplify their voices, mobilize supporters, and raise awareness about critical issues.

Vex Aleron's experience with the Kaevin Pride Parade illustrates this transformative potential. The event, initially a modest gathering, grew exponentially as younger activists utilized social media to promote it. Their ability to engage a wider audience not only increased participation but also sparked conversations about LGBTQ rights across the region. This example underscores the necessity of embracing new leadership styles and approaches to activism.

Creating a Legacy of Inclusivity

Passing the torch is not solely about transferring leadership; it is also about cultivating a culture of inclusivity within the movement. Vex Aleron recognized that the future of LGBTQ activism must be rooted in intersectionality, ensuring that all voices are heard and represented. This commitment to inclusivity involves actively seeking out and uplifting marginalized voices within the community, particularly those of LGBTQ individuals of color, transgender individuals, and those with disabilities.

By fostering an environment where diverse perspectives are valued, Vex aimed to create a legacy that future leaders could build upon. This approach not only enriches the movement but also strengthens its foundation, ensuring that it remains relevant and responsive to the needs of all community members.

Conclusion

In conclusion, the act of passing the torch to future leaders in LGBTQ activism is a multifaceted process that encompasses mentorship, education, and a commitment to inclusivity. As Vex Aleron reflects on their journey, it becomes clear that empowering the next generation is essential for the continued progress of the movement. By addressing the challenges inherent in this transition and embracing the transformative potential of new leaders, the LGBTQ community can forge a path toward a more equitable and inclusive future. The legacy of activism is not just about the battles fought but also about the leaders who will carry the torch forward, illuminating the way for generations to come.

Reflection on Personal Growth and Transformation

As Vex Aleron navigated the tumultuous waters of activism, the journey became not just a fight for LGBTQ rights but also a profound path of personal growth and transformation. This section delves into the intricate layers of Vex's evolution, highlighting the theoretical frameworks that underpin personal development, the challenges faced along the way, and the moments of epiphany that catalyzed change.

Theoretical Frameworks of Personal Growth

Personal growth can be understood through various psychological theories, including Maslow's Hierarchy of Needs and Erikson's Stages of Psychosocial Development. Maslow (1943) posits that individuals must satisfy basic needs—such as physiological, safety, love, and esteem—before achieving self-actualization, the pinnacle of personal growth. For Vex, the journey began with the struggle for acceptance and safety within a traditional society, which often marginalized LGBTQ identities.

Erikson (1950) outlines eight stages of psychosocial development, each characterized by a central conflict. Vex's experiences can be mapped onto Erikson's framework, particularly during the stages of Identity vs. Role Confusion and Intimacy vs. Isolation. The resolution of these conflicts was crucial in shaping Vex's identity and fostering connections with others, both within and outside the LGBTQ community.

Challenges Faced

The road to self-discovery was fraught with challenges. Vex encountered significant societal resistance, which often manifested as homophobia and transphobia. For instance, during high school, Vex faced bullying and ostracization from peers, leading to feelings of isolation and self-doubt. These experiences are indicative of the broader societal issues that LGBTQ individuals often face, including the internalization of stigma and the struggle for self-acceptance.

Moreover, Vex grappled with the expectations of family and community. The pressure to conform to traditional norms created a dichotomy between personal identity and societal expectations. This conflict is well-documented in LGBTQ literature, where the struggle for authenticity often leads to a painful yet transformative journey of self-acceptance (Schmitt, 2006).

Moments of Epiphany

Amidst these challenges, several pivotal moments catalyzed Vex's personal transformation. One such moment occurred during a local LGBTQ pride event. Vex witnessed the power of community as individuals came together to celebrate their identities and advocate for their rights. This experience served as a turning point, instilling a sense of belonging and purpose. The collective energy and resilience of the community provided Vex with the courage to embrace their identity fully.

Another significant moment of reflection occurred during a confrontation with a family member who held traditional views. Instead of succumbing to anger or resentment, Vex chose to engage in a heartfelt dialogue, sharing personal experiences and the importance of acceptance. This encounter not only deepened Vex's understanding of empathy but also highlighted the transformative power of communication in bridging divides.

Integration of Experiences

As Vex continued to engage in activism, the integration of these experiences into a coherent sense of self became paramount. The process of reflection involved recognizing the interplay between personal identity and activism. Vex learned that activism was not merely a political endeavor but also a deeply personal journey that required vulnerability and authenticity.

The concept of intersectionality, introduced by Crenshaw (1989), played a crucial role in Vex's understanding of personal growth. By acknowledging the multiple identities that intersect within the LGBTQ community—such as race, gender, and socioeconomic status—Vex developed a more nuanced perspective on activism. This understanding fostered a commitment to inclusivity and solidarity, recognizing that the fight for equality must encompass the diverse experiences of all individuals.

Conclusion

In conclusion, Vex Aleron's journey of personal growth and transformation is a testament to the resilience of the human spirit. Through the lens of psychological theories and lived experiences, it becomes evident that the path to self-acceptance is fraught with challenges yet rich with opportunities for growth. Vex's evolution from a marginalized individual to a recognized activist exemplifies the profound impact of community, empathy, and self-reflection in the ongoing quest for LGBTQ equality. As Vex continues to inspire others, the journey serves as a reminder that personal transformation is an essential component of collective progress in the fight for social justice.

Bibliography

[1] Maslow, A. H. (1943). A theory of human motivation. *Psychological Review*, 50(4), 370-396.

[2] Erikson, E. H. (1950). *Childhood and Society*. New York: Norton.

[3] Schmitt, J. (2006). *The Queer Movement: A History*. New York: Routledge.

[4] Crenshaw, K. (1989). Demarginalizing the intersection of race and sex: A black feminist critique of antidiscrimination doctrine, feminist theory and antiracist politics. *University of Chicago Legal Forum*, 1989(1), 139-167.

Continuing the Fight for Equality

In the ongoing struggle for LGBTQ equality, the journey does not end with victories, but rather evolves into a continuous commitment to advocacy and change. As Vex Aleron reflects on the milestones achieved, it is essential to recognize that the fight for equality is a multi-faceted endeavor, requiring persistent efforts across various domains.

The Importance of Sustained Advocacy

Advocacy is not a one-time event; it is a sustained effort that must adapt to the changing social, political, and cultural landscapes. The LGBTQ community faces a plethora of challenges that require constant vigilance and activism. For instance, while legal recognition of same-sex marriage has been achieved in many regions, issues such as discrimination in employment, housing, and healthcare persist. According to the *Williams Institute*, nearly 30% of LGBTQ individuals report experiencing discrimination in the workplace, highlighting the need for continued advocacy for comprehensive anti-discrimination laws.

Engaging New Generations

One of the key strategies for continuing the fight for equality is engaging new generations of activists. Vex emphasizes the importance of mentorship and education in fostering a new wave of leaders who are equipped to tackle the challenges ahead. Programs that focus on LGBTQ youth empowerment, such as the *Queer Youth Leadership Conference*, serve as platforms for young activists to learn from seasoned leaders, share their experiences, and develop skills necessary for effective advocacy.

Intersectionality in Activism

As the fight for LGBTQ equality progresses, it is crucial to embrace an intersectional approach that recognizes the diverse identities within the community. This includes acknowledging the unique challenges faced by LGBTQ individuals of color, transgender and non-binary individuals, and those with disabilities. The *Intersectionality Theory*, proposed by Kimberlé Crenshaw, provides a framework for understanding how various forms of discrimination intersect and compound. Vex advocates for a unified movement that amplifies the voices of marginalized groups, ensuring that the fight for equality is inclusive and representative of all experiences.

Addressing Global Inequalities

The struggle for LGBTQ rights is not confined to national borders; it is a global issue that requires international solidarity. Vex has collaborated with activists from countries where LGBTQ rights are severely restricted, such as in parts of Africa and the Middle East, to raise awareness and support for their struggles. Initiatives like *Global Equality Fund* provide resources and support to LGBTQ activists worldwide, demonstrating that the fight for equality is a shared responsibility that transcends geographical boundaries.

Utilizing Technology for Activism

In the digital age, technology plays a pivotal role in advancing the fight for equality. Social media platforms have become powerful tools for activism, enabling the rapid dissemination of information and mobilization of support. Vex has harnessed the power of platforms like Twitter and Instagram to raise awareness about LGBTQ issues, share personal stories, and organize campaigns. The use of hashtags such as

#TransRightsAreHumanRights and #BlackLivesMatter has helped create a sense of community and urgency, galvanizing support for intersectional causes.

The Role of Art and Culture

Art and culture remain vital components of the fight for equality. Vex believes that creative expression can challenge stereotypes, provoke thought, and inspire change. Initiatives that promote LGBTQ artists, such as the *Outfest Film Festival* and the *LGBTQ+ Arts Festival*, provide platforms for marginalized voices and stories, fostering a greater understanding of the diversity within the community. By celebrating LGBTQ art, activists can engage broader audiences and cultivate empathy and support for the movement.

Legislative Advocacy and Policy Change

Continuing the fight for equality also involves persistent legislative advocacy. Vex has worked closely with lawmakers to draft and promote bills that protect LGBTQ rights, such as the *Equality Act*, which seeks to amend the Civil Rights Act to prohibit discrimination based on sexual orientation and gender identity. The passage of such legislation is crucial in creating a legal framework that upholds the rights of LGBTQ individuals and safeguards against discrimination.

Building Alliances and Coalitions

Collaboration with other social justice movements is essential for the ongoing fight for LGBTQ equality. Vex has actively engaged with feminist, racial justice, and disability rights organizations to build coalitions that address systemic inequalities. By forming alliances, activists can leverage collective power to advocate for comprehensive reforms that benefit all marginalized communities.

Conclusion

In conclusion, the fight for LGBTQ equality is an enduring journey that requires unwavering commitment, adaptability, and collaboration. Vex Aleron's legacy is not merely a reflection of past achievements but a call to action for future generations. By continuing to advocate for inclusive policies, engage diverse voices, utilize technology, and foster artistic expression, the LGBTQ community can ensure that the fight for equality remains vibrant and impactful. The journey may be long, but with each step forward, the vision of a more equitable society becomes increasingly attainable.

The Power of Art and Creativity

Using Art as a Tool for Activism

Art has long been a powerful medium for expressing dissent, advocating for change, and fostering community. In the context of LGBTQ activism, art serves not only as a form of self-expression but also as a crucial tool for raising awareness, challenging societal norms, and mobilizing support. This section explores the multifaceted role of art in activism, drawing on relevant theories, addressing inherent challenges, and providing illustrative examples.

Theoretical Framework

The use of art in activism can be understood through several theoretical lenses, including cultural studies, critical theory, and social movement theory. Cultural studies emphasize the role of culture in shaping social identities and power dynamics. Art, as a cultural artifact, reflects and influences societal attitudes towards LGBTQ individuals. According to Hall (1997), representation in art is not merely about reflecting reality but is also about constructing identities and meanings. This perspective highlights how LGBTQ artists can challenge dominant narratives and create counter-narratives that affirm their identities.

Critical theory, particularly the works of Adorno and Horkheimer, suggests that culture can be a site of resistance against the commodification of human experience. Art that critiques societal norms and injustices can inspire collective action and foster critical consciousness. In this context, LGBTQ activism through art becomes a means of resisting oppression and advocating for equality.

Social movement theory posits that successful movements often rely on cultural resources to mobilize support and sustain momentum. Art can serve as a rallying point, galvanizing communities around shared experiences and goals. The emotional resonance of art can inspire individuals to engage in activism, making it an effective tool for social change.

Challenges in Utilizing Art for Activism

Despite its potential, the use of art in activism is not without challenges. One significant issue is the risk of co-optation, where mainstream culture appropriates LGBTQ art for commercial gain without supporting the underlying causes. This commodification can dilute the original message and undermine the authenticity of the activist intent. For example, Pride merchandise that commodifies LGBTQ symbols may fail to address the systemic issues faced by the community.

Another challenge is the accessibility of art. Not all LGBTQ individuals have equal access to artistic platforms, which can lead to a lack of representation within the movement. Marginalized voices, such as those of LGBTQ people of color or individuals with disabilities, may be overlooked in mainstream artistic expressions. This exclusion can perpetuate existing inequalities within the LGBTQ community and hinder the movement's overall effectiveness.

Moreover, the intersection of art and activism can sometimes lead to backlash. Artists may face censorship, harassment, or violence in response to their work, especially when it challenges deeply ingrained societal norms. This risk can deter individuals from using art as a means of activism, limiting the diversity of voices and perspectives within the movement.

Examples of Art in LGBTQ Activism

Despite these challenges, numerous examples illustrate the powerful role of art in LGBTQ activism. One notable instance is the work of Keith Haring, whose vibrant murals and public art pieces addressed issues such as AIDS awareness and LGBTQ rights during the 1980s. Haring's art transcended traditional gallery spaces, reaching a wide audience and fostering dialogue around critical issues. His iconic imagery became synonymous with activism, demonstrating how art can serve as a catalyst for social change.

Another example is the "Queer Nation" movement, which emerged in the early 1990s. This grassroots organization utilized provocative art and performance to challenge societal norms and advocate for LGBTQ rights. Their use of public demonstrations, such as the "Kiss-In" protests, highlighted the importance of visibility and representation in the fight for equality. By reclaiming public spaces through art, Queer Nation effectively engaged communities and raised awareness about LGBTQ issues.

Contemporary artists like Zanele Muholi and David Hockney continue to use their work as a means of activism. Muholi's photography focuses on the lives of LGBTQ individuals in South Africa, capturing their struggles and triumphs while challenging stereotypes. Hockney's vibrant paintings often celebrate love and relationships, contributing to the visibility of LGBTQ experiences in mainstream art. Both artists exemplify how art can serve as a powerful tool for advocacy, fostering empathy and understanding within society.

Conclusion

In conclusion, art is an invaluable tool for LGBTQ activism, offering a means of expression, resistance, and community building. By utilizing various artistic forms, activists can challenge societal norms, raise awareness, and mobilize support for their cause. While challenges such as co-optation, accessibility, and backlash persist, the transformative power of art remains a vital component of the ongoing struggle for LGBTQ equality. As history has shown, the intersection of art and activism can inspire change, foster solidarity, and ultimately contribute to a more inclusive and equitable society.

Promoting LGBTQ Artists and Performers

Promoting LGBTQ artists and performers is not just about showcasing their talents; it involves creating spaces where their voices can be heard, their stories told, and their identities celebrated. In a society that has historically marginalized LGBTQ individuals, the arts serve as a powerful platform for expression and activism. This section explores the importance of promoting LGBTQ artists, the challenges they face, and the transformative power of their contributions to culture and society.

The Importance of Representation

Representation in the arts is crucial for fostering understanding and acceptance. LGBTQ artists bring unique perspectives that challenge societal norms and broaden the narrative landscape. According to [?], representation can significantly influence public perception and foster empathy. When LGBTQ stories are told authentically, they not only validate the experiences of LGBTQ individuals but also educate broader audiences, thus promoting inclusivity.

Challenges Faced by LGBTQ Artists

Despite the progress made, LGBTQ artists still encounter numerous challenges:

- **Funding and Resources:** Many LGBTQ artists struggle to secure funding for their projects. Traditional funding bodies may be hesitant to support work that addresses LGBTQ themes, perceiving it as niche or controversial. This can lead to a lack of visibility and opportunities for these artists.

- **Censorship and Discrimination:** LGBTQ artists often face censorship from institutions that fear backlash from conservative audiences. This can stifle creativity and limit the expression of authentic narratives. For example, the case of *The Laramie Project*, a play about the murder of Matthew Shepard, faced numerous cancellations and protests, highlighting the ongoing struggle against censorship in the arts.

- **Mental Health Struggles:** The intersection of being an artist and part of the LGBTQ community can lead to unique mental health challenges. The pressure to conform to societal expectations, combined with the stigma surrounding LGBTQ identities, can exacerbate feelings of isolation and anxiety among artists [?].

Strategies for Promotion

To effectively promote LGBTQ artists and performers, several strategies can be employed:

1. **Creating Inclusive Platforms:** Establishing spaces that prioritize LGBTQ voices is essential. This includes LGBTQ-focused art festivals, galleries, and performance venues. For instance, the *Frameline Film Festival* in San Francisco has successfully showcased LGBTQ filmmakers and their stories for over four decades, providing a crucial platform for visibility.

2. **Collaboration with Established Institutions:** Partnering with mainstream institutions can amplify LGBTQ voices. Collaborations can take the form of curated exhibitions, joint performances, or educational workshops that highlight LGBTQ artists. The *Queer|Art|Mentorship* program exemplifies this approach, pairing emerging LGBTQ artists with established mentors in various artistic fields.

3. **Utilizing Social Media:** In the digital age, social media has become an invaluable tool for artists to promote their work. Platforms like Instagram and TikTok allow LGBTQ artists to reach global audiences, share their stories, and connect with supporters. Hashtags like #LGBTQArt and #PrideArt create community and visibility.

4. **Advocacy and Support:** Organizations dedicated to LGBTQ rights, such as the *Human Rights Campaign*, can play a significant role in promoting artists. These organizations can provide grants, resources, and networking opportunities to support LGBTQ creatives, ensuring their work reaches wider audiences.

Case Studies

Several LGBTQ artists have successfully navigated these challenges, serving as inspirations for future generations:

- **RuPaul:** As a drag performer and television personality, RuPaul has redefined the landscape of LGBTQ representation in mainstream media. His show, *RuPaul's Drag Race*, has not only provided a platform for drag artists but has also educated audiences about LGBTQ culture, celebrating diversity and self-expression.
- **Alok Vaid-Menon:** A gender non-conforming artist, Alok uses poetry and performance art to address issues of gender identity and societal expectations. Their work challenges binary notions of gender and highlights the experiences of marginalized communities within the LGBTQ spectrum.
- **Tegan and Sara:** This Canadian indie pop duo has used their platform to advocate for LGBTQ rights while producing music that resonates with both LGBTQ and mainstream audiences. Their visibility has helped normalize LGBTQ identities in the music industry, inspiring countless fans.

Conclusion

Promoting LGBTQ artists and performers is essential for fostering a more inclusive and empathetic society. By addressing the challenges they face and implementing strategies to amplify their voices, we can create a cultural landscape that celebrates diversity and promotes understanding. As we continue to champion LGBTQ artists, we not only enrich our cultural heritage but also pave the way for future generations to express their identities freely and authentically.

Harnessing the Power of Music, Theater, and Film

The arts have long served as a powerful vehicle for social change, and within the realm of LGBTQ activism, music, theater, and film have emerged as potent tools for advocacy, representation, and community building. These art forms not only entertain but also educate, provoke thought, and inspire action, making them invaluable in the fight for equality and acceptance.

Theoretical Framework

The intersection of art and activism is often examined through the lens of cultural theory, particularly the works of theorists like Theodor Adorno and Herbert

Marcuse, who argue that art can challenge the status quo and stimulate critical consciousness. Adorno's concept of the "culture industry" suggests that popular culture often reinforces societal norms, yet it also possesses the potential to subvert those norms by offering alternative narratives. In the context of LGBTQ activism, this means that music, theater, and film can provide counter-narratives that challenge heteronormative ideologies and promote diverse representations of identity.

Music as a Catalyst for Change

Music has historically been a rallying cry for marginalized communities, and the LGBTQ movement is no exception. From the anthems of the Stonewall Riots to contemporary pop hits celebrating queer love, music serves as both a form of expression and a means of mobilization. For instance, the song "Born This Way" by Lady Gaga became an anthem for LGBTQ youth, promoting messages of self-acceptance and pride. Its catchy chorus and infectious beat not only resonated with listeners but also catalyzed discussions around identity and belonging.

Moreover, music festivals and pride parades often feature LGBTQ artists, creating spaces where individuals can celebrate their identities openly. These events foster community solidarity and provide visibility to artists who might otherwise be marginalized in mainstream culture. The work of artists like Frank Ocean, who openly discusses his sexuality in his music, exemplifies how personal narratives can influence broader societal perceptions.

Theater as a Space for Dialogue

Theater has the unique ability to create immersive experiences that challenge audiences' perceptions and encourage empathy. Productions like *Angels in America* by Tony Kushner and *The Laramie Project* by Moisés Kaufman tackle complex themes of identity, discrimination, and the impact of the AIDS crisis. These plays not only inform audiences about LGBTQ issues but also humanize the struggles faced by the community, fostering understanding and compassion.

Moreover, community theater initiatives often engage local LGBTQ populations, providing a platform for voices that are frequently silenced. For example, the *Queer Theater Project* in various cities invites LGBTQ individuals to share their stories, thus reclaiming narratives and promoting visibility. This grassroots approach not only empowers participants but also enriches the cultural landscape by introducing diverse perspectives.

Film: Shaping Perceptions and Narratives

Film serves as a powerful medium for storytelling, capable of reaching vast audiences and shaping societal norms. Movies like *Moonlight* and *Call Me by Your Name* have garnered critical acclaim for their nuanced portrayals of LGBTQ relationships, challenging stereotypes and offering authentic representations of queer love. These films not only entertain but also educate viewers about the complexities of identity and desire.

However, the representation of LGBTQ individuals in film has historically been fraught with challenges. The "bury your gays" trope, where LGBTQ characters are killed off to further the plot of heterosexual characters, reflects a troubling pattern in Hollywood. Activists have called for more responsible storytelling that prioritizes authentic representation and avoids harmful clichés. The success of films like *Love, Simon* demonstrates that there is a demand for positive LGBTQ narratives, prompting a shift in the industry towards more inclusive storytelling.

Challenges and Opportunities

While the arts provide a platform for LGBTQ activism, challenges remain. Issues of funding, access, and representation persist, particularly for LGBTQ artists of color and those from lower socioeconomic backgrounds. The commercialization of pride events and the appropriation of queer culture by mainstream media can dilute the original messages of resistance and solidarity.

To combat these challenges, it is crucial for activists and artists to collaborate, ensuring that the narratives presented are authentic and inclusive. Initiatives like the *LGBTQ Film Festival* and community arts programs play a vital role in supporting emerging artists and amplifying diverse voices. By harnessing the power of music, theater, and film, the LGBTQ movement can continue to inspire change, educate the public, and foster a sense of belonging within the community.

Conclusion

In conclusion, music, theater, and film are not merely forms of entertainment; they are powerful tools for activism that can shape perceptions, challenge societal norms, and foster community. By leveraging these art forms, LGBTQ activists can create spaces for dialogue, promote visibility, and inspire future generations to continue the fight for equality. As we navigate the complexities of identity and representation, it is essential to recognize the transformative potential of the arts in advancing the cause of LGBTQ rights and inclusivity.

Exploring Intersectional LGBTQ Representation in Art

The intersectionality of LGBTQ representation in art is a crucial area of exploration that reflects the diverse identities and experiences within the LGBTQ community. Intersectionality, a term coined by Kimberlé Crenshaw, emphasizes how various social identities—such as race, gender, sexuality, and class—interact to create unique modes of discrimination and privilege. In the context of LGBTQ representation, it is essential to consider how these intersecting identities shape artistic expression and the narratives that emerge from them.

Theoretical Framework

To understand intersectional representation in art, we must first acknowledge the foundational theories that underpin it. Intersectionality serves as a lens through which we can analyze how marginalized identities are portrayed in various art forms. The work of scholars such as bell hooks and Audre Lorde further enriches this discourse by emphasizing the importance of including voices from all corners of the LGBTQ spectrum, particularly those who are often silenced due to their intersecting identities.

For instance, hooks (1992) argues that the representation of Black women in media and art is often fraught with stereotypes and misrepresentations. This critique can be extended to LGBTQ art, where artists of color, transgender individuals, and those with disabilities frequently encounter barriers in achieving visibility. The need for a more inclusive narrative is paramount, as it allows for a richer tapestry of experiences to be woven into the cultural fabric.

Challenges in Representation

Despite the growing awareness of intersectionality, numerous challenges persist in achieving authentic representation of LGBTQ individuals in art. One significant issue is the prevalence of tokenism, where artists or characters from marginalized groups are included merely to fulfill diversity quotas rather than to provide meaningful representation. This often leads to one-dimensional portrayals that fail to capture the complexities of their identities.

Moreover, the art world is often dominated by mainstream narratives that prioritize certain voices over others. For example, white cisgender gay men have historically received more visibility and support within the LGBTQ art scene, overshadowing the contributions of queer people of color and transgender artists. This disparity not only limits the scope of artistic expression but also perpetuates harmful stereotypes that marginalize already underrepresented groups.

Examples of Intersectional Representation

Despite these challenges, there are numerous examples of artists and movements that successfully embrace intersectional LGBTQ representation. One notable figure is the artist Zanele Muholi, a South African photographer whose work focuses on the lives of Black LGBTQ individuals. Muholi's series "Faces and Phases" captures the diverse identities within the LGBTQ community, challenging stereotypes and celebrating the beauty of queer existence.

Another poignant example is the work of the late Marsha P. Johnson, a Black transgender activist and artist who played a pivotal role in the Stonewall uprising. Johnson's art and activism were deeply intertwined, as she used her creative expression to advocate for the rights of marginalized LGBTQ individuals. Her legacy continues to inspire contemporary artists who seek to honor the intersectional nature of their identities.

In literature, authors such as Ocean Vuong and Jesmyn Ward explore the complexities of intersecting identities in their narratives. Vuong's poetry, which often reflects on his Vietnamese heritage and queer identity, showcases the beauty of blending personal history with broader societal issues. Similarly, Ward's novels delve into the experiences of Black characters navigating their sexual identities in a world that often marginalizes them.

The Role of Art in Activism

Art serves as a powerful tool for activism, particularly in the context of intersectional LGBTQ representation. By amplifying the voices of marginalized artists and storytellers, we can challenge dominant narratives and foster a more inclusive understanding of the LGBTQ experience. Community art projects, such as murals and public installations, provide spaces for collective expression and healing, allowing individuals to share their stories and connect with others who share similar experiences.

Furthermore, social media platforms have revolutionized the way intersectional LGBTQ art is disseminated and consumed. Artists can now reach global audiences, bypassing traditional gatekeepers of the art world. This democratization of art allows for a broader range of voices to be heard, fostering a sense of community and solidarity among marginalized groups.

Conclusion

Exploring intersectional LGBTQ representation in art is essential for creating a more inclusive and nuanced understanding of the diverse experiences within the community. By acknowledging the complexities of identity and advocating for authentic representation, we can challenge stereotypes, combat discrimination, and celebrate the rich tapestry of LGBTQ lives. As we continue to elevate the voices of marginalized artists, we pave the way for a future where all identities are recognized and valued in the artistic realm. The journey toward intersectional representation is ongoing, but through art, we can inspire change and foster understanding across the spectrum of human experience.

Inspiring Change through Creative Expression

The intersection of art and activism has long been a powerful catalyst for social change, particularly within the LGBTQ community. Creative expression serves not only as a form of personal liberation but also as a means of challenging societal norms and advocating for equality. This section delves into the various ways in which art can inspire change, highlighting relevant theories, challenges, and notable examples.

Theoretical Framework

Art as activism is grounded in several theoretical frameworks, including Critical Theory and Social Movement Theory. Critical Theory posits that art can be a tool for critiquing societal structures and ideologies, enabling marginalized voices to articulate their experiences and struggles. Social Movement Theory, on the other hand, emphasizes the role of collective identity and cultural production in mobilizing communities for social change.

$$\text{Artistic Expression} \to \text{Social Awareness} \to \text{Activism} \qquad (42)$$

This equation encapsulates the transformative process by which artistic expression fosters social awareness, ultimately leading to activism. Through this lens, art becomes a vehicle for social justice, providing a platform for LGBTQ narratives that challenge dominant discourses.

Challenges in Creative Expression

While art has the potential to inspire change, it is not without its challenges. LGBTQ artists often face systemic barriers, including censorship, lack of funding, and societal discrimination. These obstacles can hinder their ability to produce and share their work. Additionally, the commercialization of art can dilute its activist potential, leading to a focus on aesthetics over message.

Moreover, the intersectionality of identity plays a crucial role in the challenges faced by LGBTQ artists. Artists who identify as people of color, transgender, or disabled often encounter compounded discrimination, making it essential to create inclusive spaces that amplify diverse voices.

Examples of Art as Activism

Numerous examples illustrate how art has been effectively utilized as a tool for activism within the LGBTQ community. One notable instance is the work of the late artist Keith Haring, whose vibrant murals addressed issues such as AIDS awareness and LGBTQ visibility. Haring's art transcended traditional boundaries, engaging the public in conversations about stigma and discrimination.

Another powerful example is the documentary film *Paris is Burning*, which provides an intimate look at the drag ball culture of the 1980s in New York City. The film not only celebrates LGBTQ identity and resilience but also critiques the systemic racism and classism that permeate society. By documenting the lives of its subjects, the film serves as both an artistic expression and a historical record, inspiring subsequent generations to continue the fight for equality.

The Role of Music and Performance

Music and performance art have also played significant roles in LGBTQ activism. The emergence of queer music genres, such as disco and punk, has historically provided a soundtrack for resistance. Artists like Madonna and Lady Gaga have used their platforms to advocate for LGBTQ rights, embedding messages of empowerment and acceptance within their music.

Performance art, exemplified by figures like Marina Abramović, challenges audiences to confront uncomfortable truths about identity and society. Abramović's work often blurs the lines between performer and audience, creating immersive experiences that invite reflection on personal and collective identity.

Community Engagement through Art

Artistic initiatives that engage the community can foster solidarity and inspire change. Programs like *The Queer Arts Festival* in Vancouver highlight the importance of creating spaces for LGBTQ artists to showcase their work and connect with audiences. Such festivals not only promote visibility but also encourage dialogue about pressing social issues.

Moreover, community-based art projects, such as murals and public installations, can serve as powerful symbols of resistance and pride. These projects often involve collaboration between artists and local LGBTQ organizations, ensuring that the voices of marginalized communities are represented and heard.

Conclusion

In conclusion, creative expression is a vital component of LGBTQ activism, serving as both a means of personal liberation and a tool for social change. By harnessing the power of art, LGBTQ individuals can challenge societal norms, inspire empathy, and mobilize communities for justice. Despite the challenges faced by LGBTQ artists, their contributions to the movement are invaluable, shaping the narrative of equality and inclusion for future generations.

$$\text{Art} + \text{Activism} = \text{Social Change} \tag{43}$$

Ultimately, the fusion of art and activism not only enriches the LGBTQ movement but also paves the way for a more inclusive and equitable society.

Bibliography

[1] Meyer, I. H. (2003). Prejudice, social stress, and mental health in gay populations: Conceptual issues and research evidence. *Psychological Bulletin*, 129(5), 674-697.

[2] Ryan, C., Huebner, D., Diaz, R. M., & Sanchez, J. (2009). Family acceptance in adolescence and the health of LGBT young adults. *Journal of Child and Adolescent Psychiatric Nursing*, 22(4), 205-213.

[3] Cohen, S., & Wills, T. A. (1985). Stress, social support, and the buffering hypothesis. *Psychological Bulletin*, 98(2), 310-357.

Index

-doubt, 173

a, 3–5, 7–19, 21–26, 28–31, 34, 36–38, 40, 42, 43, 45–49, 51–58, 60, 61, 64–70, 73–78, 80, 82, 84, 85, 87–91, 93–95, 97–100, 102–113, 115–117, 119, 121, 122, 124, 125, 127, 128, 130–132, 134–148, 151, 153–158, 160–163, 165–175, 178–180, 182–189
ability, 25, 26, 43, 48, 58, 124, 144, 147, 172, 187
absence, 69, 90, 93
abuse, 22, 156
acceptance, 3, 5, 8, 9, 15, 16, 25, 29, 40, 49, 52, 53, 56–58, 76, 120, 137, 138, 155, 173, 174, 182, 183, 188
access, 47, 104, 112, 128, 141, 148, 156, 179, 184
accessibility, 139, 179, 180
accountability, 99
achievement, 29, 105, 110
act, 18, 37, 66, 70, 122, 158, 160, 166, 172

action, 13, 15, 18, 38, 40, 45, 49, 53, 59, 84, 100, 102, 111, 113, 115, 130, 170, 178, 182
activism, 5, 9, 13–18, 21, 22, 24–26, 29, 31, 36–38, 40, 43, 45–49, 53–56, 61, 64–68, 70, 80, 84, 88, 89, 91, 93–95, 97, 100, 102, 105, 111, 117, 122, 125, 127, 133, 135, 137–140, 142–145, 147–149, 151, 153, 154, 158–160, 163, 165, 167–172, 174, 178–180, 182–184, 186–189
activist, 13–15, 17, 21, 24, 26, 31, 54, 58, 65, 67, 68, 90, 94, 95, 110, 128, 149, 151, 157, 158, 174, 178, 187
adaptability, 88, 144
addition, 8, 171
address, 31, 45, 47, 49, 51, 56–58, 130, 136, 154, 157, 165, 177, 178
adjustment, 68
adolescence, 8
Adorno, 183
advancement, 142, 156

adversary, 89
adversity, 18, 24, 26, 30, 43, 45, 49, 97
advice, 141
advisory, 110
advocacy, 13, 22, 23, 40, 42, 58, 64, 77, 78, 80, 84, 87, 108, 110, 111, 119, 122, 130, 147, 149, 153, 154, 161, 165, 167–169, 171, 175, 179, 182
advocate, 24–27, 38, 40, 45, 56, 58, 73, 82, 84, 105, 108, 111, 112, 135, 137–139, 147, 165, 169, 174, 177, 179, 188
affirmation, 57
aftermath, 18, 53
age, 38, 142, 145, 149
agency, 48
agreement, 139
Alex, 94, 95
alienation, 4, 99, 157
allyship, 14, 26, 46, 47, 55, 56
ambition, 26, 103, 105
amount, 48
anger, 174
animosity, 136
announcement, 145
anonymity, 145
anthem, 183
anticipation, 105, 110
anxiety, 3, 30, 110
appreciation, 167
approach, 8, 11, 36, 42, 49, 52, 56, 57, 64, 75, 82, 84, 89, 90, 97, 105, 106, 108, 110, 111, 128, 136, 139, 143, 153, 155, 157, 172

appropriation, 184
argument, 95
art, 8, 178–180, 182–189
artist, 188
aspect, 9, 31, 43, 49, 56, 64, 68, 76, 84, 95, 117, 137, 160, 169
aspiration, 168
assembly, 13
asset, 144
assistance, 47
assurance, 171
atmosphere, 23, 28, 53, 57
attachment, 71
attendance, 109
attention, 15, 18, 23, 66, 167
audience, 37, 42, 104, 147, 172, 179
Audre Lorde, 185
authenticity, 3, 5, 10, 120, 121, 174, 178
awakening, 14
awareness, 17, 18, 30, 48, 51, 58, 84, 87–89, 140, 151, 164, 166, 172, 178–180, 185, 187, 188

backdrop, 5
background, 153
backing, 114
backlash, 13, 23, 25, 26, 34, 45, 49, 94, 111, 143, 145, 167, 179, 180
balance, 67, 68, 90, 99, 130
barrier, 13, 57, 148
base, 58
battle, 21–24, 53, 66, 97
battlefield, 30
battleground, 58
beacon, 5, 26, 105, 165
beat, 183

Index 195

beauty, 64
bedrock, 133
beginning, 5, 24, 110
behavioral, 48
being, 8, 15, 17, 30, 45, 53, 57, 58, 67, 70, 76, 90, 91, 94, 95, 107, 116, 145, 158
belief, 31, 110
bell, 185
belonging, 4, 16, 37, 139, 166, 169, 170, 174, 183
benefit, 111, 177
bias, 117–119, 144
bill, 23, 24
board, 110
book, 8, 9
breakthrough, 105
breeding, 89
bridging, 133, 174
brunt, 93
buffer, 48, 66
building, 16, 22, 23, 30, 31, 37, 50, 60, 89, 97, 106–108, 110, 111, 130, 132, 134, 138, 165, 171, 180, 182
bulletin, 52
bullying, 145, 173
burden, 97
burnout, 89–91
business, 138
bystander, 40

camaraderie, 11
campaign, 30, 52, 104, 106, 109, 136
campaigning, 29
campus, 34, 36
candidacy, 29, 105, 107
capital, 111, 113, 128
care, 66, 68, 90, 91, 156

career, 103, 156
case, 137, 144, 145
catalyst, 26, 166, 179, 187
cause, 48, 52, 94, 131, 180, 184
celebration, 16, 36, 51
censorship, 179, 187
challenge, 17, 19, 21, 22, 26, 38, 40, 47, 48, 51, 56, 57, 66, 69, 70, 80, 98, 105, 108, 116, 117, 119, 120, 125, 139, 142, 155, 156, 171, 179, 180, 183, 184, 186, 187, 189
change, 5, 15, 16, 18, 23, 24, 26, 31, 39, 43, 49, 51, 53, 57, 58, 66, 69, 70, 80, 84, 89, 102, 103, 105, 107, 110, 113, 125, 127, 130, 132, 137, 139, 140, 142, 144, 151, 165, 167, 173, 175, 178–180, 182, 187, 189
changer, 8
chaos, 64
chapter, 29
Charles Tilly, 15
check, 68
checking, 143
childhood, 94
choice, 15, 57
chorus, 183
cisgender, 163, 185
city, 51–53, 109, 112
clarity, 68
clash, 4
class, 47, 128, 158, 163
Classism, 47
classism, 45
club, 8, 9
co, 178, 180

coalition, 22, 30, 51, 106, 110, 111, 130, 132, 139, 171
collaboration, 34, 37, 38, 47, 57, 65, 86–89, 111, 112, 128, 130–132, 136–139, 146, 165, 169, 189
collapse, 23
collective, 13, 15, 16, 18, 25, 30, 36, 40, 43, 45, 47–49, 53, 56, 58, 71, 84, 89, 100, 102, 111, 113, 115, 130, 132, 139, 165, 174, 177, 178, 186, 187
color, 21, 34, 46, 52, 106, 130, 138, 139, 147, 153–157, 163, 167, 169, 172, 179, 184, 185, 188
combat, 39, 48, 59, 60, 72, 80, 81, 91, 98, 118, 119, 143, 145, 187
combination, 42, 73
commercialization, 167, 184, 187
commitment, 14, 23, 29, 34, 47–49, 56, 67, 87, 89, 93–95, 107, 110, 112, 121, 127, 132, 134, 136–138, 170–172, 175
committee, 52, 53
commodification, 178
communication, 85, 95, 111, 142, 174
community, 3, 5, 8–10, 13–18, 22, 24, 26–31, 34–38, 40, 42, 45–55, 57, 58, 60, 65–67, 70, 72, 73, 85, 91, 95, 97–103, 105–108, 110–112, 115, 117, 127, 130, 135, 136, 138–140, 142–145, 147–149, 154, 157, 161–174, 178–180, 182–184, 186–188
companionship, 74, 76
compassion, 56, 139
component, 33, 42, 73, 80, 166, 174, 180, 189
compound, 160
concealment, 10
concept, 31, 71, 97, 111, 137, 139, 170, 183
concern, 64, 94
conclusion, 33, 47, 49, 70, 84, 89, 95, 105, 107, 111, 130, 144, 149, 157, 167, 170, 172, 174, 180, 184, 189
confidence, 171
conflict, 3, 95, 124
conformity, 7
confrontation, 174
confusion, 4
connection, 9, 69, 73, 94
consciousness, 178, 183
content, 25, 120, 121, 142, 144, 146, 147
contention, 95
context, 16, 21, 43, 111, 135, 145, 163, 171, 178, 183, 186
contrast, 40
control, 40
conversation, 3, 16, 18, 95
coping, 30, 40, 45, 48, 91, 97
core, 21, 97
cornerstone, 16, 36, 102
council, 108–110, 112
counter, 30, 49, 53, 117, 141, 143, 183
courage, 19, 49, 97, 105, 168, 174
coverage, 18, 118
creation, 52, 121

Index 197

creative, 8, 144, 189
creativity, 42
credibility, 40, 107
criticism, 122, 124
crowd, 53
crucible, 29
cry, 183
culmination, 105, 110
cultivation, 26, 36
culture, 3, 13, 16, 40, 47, 49, 61, 105, 139, 167, 172, 178, 180, 183, 184
curricula, 171
curriculum, 8
cyberbullying, 145, 146, 148

date, 52
David Hockney, 179
day, 28, 53, 84, 105, 110
debate, 78, 107, 141
decision, 3, 5, 15, 94, 103
declaration, 18, 103
decline, 90
dedication, 64, 105
defeat, 90
defense, 97, 122
defiance, 18, 53, 107
demand, 18, 51, 139
democratization, 121, 186
demographic, 155
departure, 106
design, 52
desire, 3, 13, 15
despair, 49
determination, 29, 40, 45, 80, 168
deterrent, 26
development, 36, 37, 42, 71, 76, 100, 170, 173

dialogue, 29, 47, 49, 53, 56–58, 89, 95, 106, 110, 122, 124, 135–139, 174, 179, 184
dignity, 21, 24
disability, 22, 161, 165, 177
disadvantage, 128, 163
disco, 188
discomfort, 94
disconnect, 98
discord, 138
discourse, 105–107, 185
discovery, 3, 7, 14, 173
discrimination, 16, 18, 21, 22, 31, 34, 38, 40, 43, 48, 54, 70, 82, 87, 90, 109–112, 116, 117, 128, 139, 141, 154–158, 160, 161, 163, 187, 188
discussion, 9, 105, 110
disparity, 156, 185
dissemination, 84
dissent, 178
distance, 93–95
diversity, 9, 15, 22, 37, 47, 111, 120, 135, 136, 138, 139, 163–166, 169, 170, 179, 182, 185
divide, 141, 148, 149
division, 104, 137
doubt, 173
doxxing, 148
duality, 10, 15

Eastern Europe, 88
education, 14, 22, 24, 42, 47, 49, 56, 58, 73, 124, 138, 143, 149, 156, 168, 170, 172
effect, 16, 18, 26, 89, 138, 145, 171

effectiveness, 16, 33, 68, 84, 85, 148, 162, 163, 179
efficiency, 147
effort, 40, 47, 49, 56, 66, 77, 112, 130
election, 28, 105
element, 91
emergence, 171, 188
empathy, 49, 57, 69, 70, 130, 133, 134, 137, 174, 179, 189
emphasis, 135
employment, 22, 112, 156
empowerment, 5, 8, 139, 188
encounter, 13, 69, 74, 97, 101, 131, 138, 154, 158, 174, 180, 188
encouragement, 8, 66
end, 97, 175
endeavor, 58, 61, 73, 80, 113, 121, 170, 174, 175
energy, 139, 174
enforcement, 53
engagement, 8, 9, 13, 14, 23, 25, 26, 29, 31, 42, 58, 61, 88, 89, 110, 111, 122, 124, 127, 136, 142, 144, 149, 151, 166–170
entertainment, 184
enthusiasm, 139, 166
environment, 8, 14, 29, 33, 34, 36–38, 40, 42, 45–47, 49, 56, 65, 73, 105, 108, 119, 124, 137, 158, 165, 168, 172
epiphany, 173
equality, 5, 8, 9, 13–16, 24, 29–31, 34, 36, 38, 42, 45, 49, 50, 53, 56–59, 61, 64, 66, 68, 70, 73, 77–80, 82, 84, 87, 89, 91, 95, 97, 105, 107, 108, 110–113, 115–117, 119, 128, 130, 132, 134, 136–138, 141, 144, 149, 151, 155, 157, 160, 162, 163, 165, 168–170, 174, 175, 177–180, 182, 184, 187, 189
equation, 8, 9, 25, 48, 58, 88–90, 127, 130, 132, 135, 136, 154, 156, 169, 187
equilibrium, 68
equity, 47
erasure, 70, 167
erosion, 110
Erving Goffman, 15
essence, 9, 105, 130, 132, 154
establishment, 97, 107
esteem, 145
evaluation, 33, 34
event, 16, 17, 35, 40, 52, 53, 57, 172, 173
evidence, 110
evolution, 61, 170, 173, 174
example, 3, 45, 49, 52, 56, 57, 68, 88, 94, 110, 116, 135, 138, 139, 146, 156, 161, 164, 165, 167, 171, 172, 178, 179, 185
exception, 183
exchange, 71
excitement, 13, 51
exclusion, 161, 179
exercise, 155
existence, 4, 18
expansion, 61, 62, 64
expense, 3
experience, 4, 5, 14, 16, 21, 22, 29, 31, 34, 40, 69, 73, 90, 95,

139, 155–158, 161, 163, 172, 174, 178, 186, 187
expertise, 138
expression, 144, 178, 180, 183, 185–187, 189

fabric, 21, 45, 54
face, 18, 24, 26, 30, 34, 43, 45, 49, 50, 74, 76, 93, 95, 97, 107, 116, 130, 143, 148, 150, 154, 156–158, 160, 161, 163, 164, 166, 173, 179, 180, 182, 187
facet, 153
fact, 143
failing, 22
failure, 90
fairness, 162
faith, 57, 135, 137
fame, 97
family, 3, 4, 11, 23, 93, 136, 174
favor, 110
fear, 3, 10, 30, 34, 46, 103, 104, 110, 111, 135, 156, 157
feature, 183
feedback, 25
feeling, 95, 157
feminist, 177
fight, 5, 9, 13, 14, 16, 19, 21, 24, 30, 31, 38, 40, 42, 45, 49, 56, 58, 64, 65, 77, 80, 82, 84, 87, 88, 91, 95, 97, 105, 107, 110, 114–116, 119, 128, 130–132, 134, 138, 144, 149, 151, 154, 155, 157, 162, 165, 169, 170, 172, 174, 175, 177, 179, 182, 184
fighting, 15, 93, 154

figure, 16, 67
film, 16, 182–184
finding, 64, 66, 100, 112, 137, 139
firsthand, 90
Florida, 40
fluidity, 12
flyer, 17
focus, 84, 104, 112, 138, 167, 187
following, 81, 85, 86, 132
force, 134
forefront, 24, 158
form, 47, 60, 70, 131, 178, 183, 187
formation, 139
formula, 100
forum, 145
foster, 17, 26, 40, 47, 53, 56–58, 69, 70, 73, 74, 112, 117, 119, 124, 125, 133, 136, 139, 142, 149, 160, 162, 165, 168, 169, 178, 180, 183, 184, 186, 187
foundation, 14, 24, 135, 136, 139, 172
fragmentation, 138
framework, 15, 22, 31, 52, 85, 108, 110, 139, 145, 153, 161
Frank Ocean, 183
frequency, 25
friction, 138
friend, 94
friendship, 94
front, 30, 111, 128, 130
fulfillment, 73
function, 48, 154, 156
funding, 184, 187
fundraising, 47, 106
fusion, 189
future, 5, 14, 16, 19, 24, 26, 29, 31, 53, 89, 97, 105, 108, 124,

128, 137, 149, 165,
    167–172, 182, 184, 187,
    189

gain, 178
gallery, 179
game, 8
gathering, 3, 8, 23, 51, 172
gay, 116, 138, 163, 185
gender, 3, 9, 15, 22, 29, 31, 47, 56,
    110, 113, 128, 131, 135,
    137, 138, 153, 156, 158,
    161, 163
generation, 24, 36, 105, 107, 110,
    168–170, 172
gesture, 170
globe, 149
goal, 24, 110, 119, 137–139
governance, 105, 107, 108, 110
government, 17, 108, 111
ground, 56, 58, 89, 112, 135, 137,
    139
groundwork, 29, 31, 53, 105, 108
group, 9, 15, 53, 156, 166
growth, 5, 14, 47, 122, 168, 169,
    172, 174
guest, 13, 16
guidance, 74, 168
guide, 36
guilt, 67
gun, 40

hall, 112
hand, 187
harassment, 13, 26, 30, 38, 40, 95,
    97, 142, 148, 149, 179
hardship, 13
Haring, 179, 188
harm, 54

Harvey Milk, 17
hate, 40, 42, 53, 141, 143, 145, 146,
    148
hatred, 49
head, 46, 54, 56, 80, 104, 110
healing, 9, 47, 186
health, 24, 30, 57, 89–91, 97, 141,
    145, 148, 156, 167
healthcare, 22, 47, 104, 112, 138,
    156
heart, 21, 31, 51, 95, 160
help, 55, 95
helplessness, 48
Herbert Marcuse, 183
heritage, 182
heteronormativity, 3
highlight, 40, 117, 128, 131
history, 8, 16, 100, 167, 180
Hockney, 179
homelessness, 22, 57
hometown, 24
homophobia, 13, 17, 22, 40, 45,
    53–56, 80–82, 87, 103,
    117–119, 173
homosexuality, 22
hope, 5, 26, 80, 105, 163, 165
Horkheimer, 178
hostility, 13, 29, 43
housing, 22, 47, 112
hurdle, 103

idea, 49, 51, 53, 169
identity, 3–5, 8, 9, 12, 14, 15, 22, 29,
    31, 36, 37, 51, 56, 61, 64,
    67, 68, 70, 110, 135, 137,
    138, 153–156, 166, 174,
    183, 184, 187, 188
imagery, 179
imitation, 145

Index 201

impact, 26, 30, 36, 40, 45, 52, 53, 56, 57, 63, 69, 88, 89, 109, 111, 116, 118, 127, 139, 142–144, 148, 149, 171, 174
imperative, 64, 76, 110, 122, 160, 167
implementation, 31, 151
importance, 13, 14, 16, 18, 23, 24, 26, 28–31, 36, 37, 46, 47, 49, 51–53, 55, 57, 59, 60, 66, 68, 80, 84, 85, 88, 89, 91, 97, 105–107, 110, 111, 115, 124, 128, 130, 134, 138, 141, 146, 158, 163, 165, 167–171, 174, 179, 180, 185
in, 3–5, 7–10, 13–18, 21–26, 28–31, 34, 36–38, 40, 43, 45–58, 60, 61, 63, 65–70, 74–76, 78–82, 84, 85, 87–91, 93–95, 97–122, 124, 125, 127, 128, 130, 132–142, 144–149, 151, 153–162, 164–172, 174, 178, 179, 182–188
inaction, 42
inadequacy, 67, 90
incident, 40, 53
inclusion, 108, 110, 135, 158, 161, 162, 164, 166, 189
inclusivity, 25, 27, 29, 34, 36, 47, 52, 56, 64, 104, 107, 121, 132, 139, 141, 142, 153, 157, 163, 171, 172, 184
income, 47
increase, 88, 130
individual, 5, 10, 15, 16, 34, 45, 58, 70, 110, 153, 156, 174
industry, 122, 183
inequality, 54, 104, 156
inequity, 148
influence, 48, 116, 117, 128, 183
information, 42, 84, 125, 136, 141
initiative, 16, 46, 47, 49, 139, 146, 168, 171
injustice, 16, 54, 84, 90, 165
innovation, 61
insecurity, 156
insight, 104
inspiration, 81
instability, 156
instance, 22, 37, 40, 48, 49, 56, 57, 84, 87, 93, 95, 107, 112, 117, 131, 135, 136, 138, 139, 141, 154, 156, 163, 166, 168–170, 173, 179, 183, 188
institution, 26
integration, 147, 171, 174
integrity, 162
intelligence, 49, 146
intent, 103, 178
interconnectedness, 22, 80, 89
internalization, 173
internet, 141, 142, 145, 148
interplay, 5, 67, 153, 174
intersection, 64, 155, 160, 179, 180, 182, 187
intersectionality, 15, 21, 31, 34, 52, 61, 80, 82, 104, 128, 130, 138, 139, 153, 155, 157, 158, 161, 163, 169, 171, 172, 185, 188
intervention, 40
intolerance, 40
invisibility, 34

involvement, 8, 13, 16, 36, 94, 145, 146
isolation, 4, 30, 69, 90, 93, 98, 157, 161, 173
issue, 38, 78, 111, 148, 178, 185

job, 47, 156
Johnson, 157
joining, 15, 16, 131
journaling, 68
journey, 3, 5, 7, 9, 14–16, 18, 19, 21, 24, 26, 29, 31, 34, 36, 38, 48, 49, 51, 53, 56, 58, 64, 66, 68, 74, 84, 89–91, 93, 95, 97, 100, 102, 103, 105, 107, 110, 113, 117, 130, 132, 137, 155, 165, 170, 172, 174, 175, 187
joy, 53, 73
judgment, 46, 135
Judith Butler, 22
justice, 8, 14, 18, 22, 23, 46, 68, 95, 97, 104, 110, 111, 128, 131, 132, 135, 137, 142, 151, 155, 165, 174, 177, 187, 189
justification, 135

Kaevin, 25
Keith Haring, 179, 188
Kimberlé Crenshaw, 15, 21, 31, 128, 130, 139, 153, 158, 161, 163
knowledge, 14, 38, 84–87, 170, 171

labyrinth, 58
lack, 13, 51, 69, 90, 116, 156, 179, 187
Lady Gaga, 183, 188
landmark, 110

landscape, 11, 17, 22, 25, 26, 36, 40, 58, 61, 69, 80, 91, 95, 97, 103, 105, 107, 108, 111, 119–121, 125, 128, 130, 135, 137, 140–145, 147, 149, 151, 158, 168, 171, 182
language, 47, 58
law, 53, 115
lead, 21, 23, 49, 53, 56, 89, 94, 98, 99, 110, 116, 122, 128, 130, 135, 139, 141, 148, 154, 156, 157, 161, 165, 171, 179
leader, 26, 29, 31, 110
leadership, 16, 25, 29, 37, 64, 112, 164, 171, 172
learning, 34, 87, 168
legacy, 38, 107, 168, 172
legalization, 116
legislation, 40, 84, 110, 112–115, 139
lens, 174, 182, 185, 187
lesson, 8
level, 5, 25, 89
leverage, 26, 111, 125, 138, 142, 177
liberation, 187, 189
library, 8, 9
life, 5, 10, 13, 16, 29, 66–68, 95, 137
lifeline, 141
literature, 8
love, 21, 23, 24, 28, 52, 56–58, 64–66, 69, 70, 73, 74, 76, 136, 137, 139, 154, 179, 183

Madonna, 188
mainstream, 69, 117, 167, 178, 179, 183–185

majority, 105, 110
making, 117, 128, 135, 164, 178, 182, 188
man, 163
management, 66
maneuver, 122
mantle, 171
marginalization, 22, 154, 155, 157, 160
marketing, 167
marriage, 3, 23, 112, 116, 136, 141
Marsha P. Johnson, 157
Martin Luther King Jr., 17
matter, 24, 26, 66, 162
means, 9, 34, 117, 139, 145, 161, 164, 178–180, 183, 187, 189
mechanism, 165, 170
media, 17, 18, 30, 37, 38, 42, 49, 52, 69, 87, 106, 116–122, 125–128, 140–142, 145, 147, 151, 172, 184, 186
meditation, 68
medium, 178
meeting, 23, 154
member, 174
mentorship, 8, 36, 38, 84, 168, 170–172
merchandise, 178
message, 26, 36, 38, 57, 106, 125, 138, 178, 187
microcosm, 16
milestone, 24, 28, 110, 113
mindfulness, 68
minority, 71, 105
miscommunication, 130
misconception, 22
misinformation, 22, 23, 30, 31, 40, 42, 110, 141–143

misrepresentation, 69, 116, 117
mission, 73, 97, 100
misunderstanding, 30, 49, 116
mix, 108, 110
mixture, 51
mobilization, 14, 64, 88, 106, 149, 183
model, 71, 97
moment, 3, 10, 13, 16, 24, 110, 173, 174
momentum, 23, 107, 109, 144, 166, 167, 178
monolith, 163
motivation, 165
move, 103, 121, 134, 142
movement, 13, 16, 23, 25, 36, 40, 42, 45, 49, 56–59, 61–64, 67, 80, 82, 84, 85, 87, 89, 94, 98, 99, 107, 110, 124, 130, 138, 139, 142, 143, 153, 155, 157, 158, 160–163, 165–167, 169–172, 178, 179, 183, 189
movie, 11
Muholi, 179
multitude, 153
music, 182–184, 188
myriad, 74, 158

narrative, 5, 15, 16, 24, 25, 29, 38, 45, 46, 48, 49, 189
nation, 77
nature, 8, 15, 39, 40, 95, 116, 128, 141, 163
navigation, 151
necessity, 12, 24, 43, 48, 60, 98, 137, 138, 158, 165, 172
need, 3, 9, 17, 18, 40, 47, 53, 88, 90, 148, 157, 160

negativity, 48, 49
neglect, 94
network, 26, 37, 45, 48, 60, 65, 68, 99
news, 18, 118
night, 11
nightclub, 40
non, 17, 128, 130, 138, 158–160, 164
norm, 7
notion, 116
numerator, 48
nurturing, 8, 37, 66, 68, 70, 91, 94, 168

obligation, 165
observation, 145
office, 103, 105, 107
on, 5, 8, 9, 15, 16, 21, 22, 24, 25, 30, 31, 34, 37, 40, 45, 46, 49, 50, 52–54, 56, 57, 65, 67, 69, 78, 80, 84, 89, 90, 93, 95, 97, 104–106, 109, 110, 112, 116, 130, 135, 138, 139, 143–145, 153, 155, 158, 163, 167, 170–172, 175, 178, 179, 187
one, 9–11, 16, 28, 47, 48, 68, 77, 88, 98, 105, 130, 153, 162, 165, 185
onslaught, 48
openness, 10
opinion, 110
opposition, 15, 17, 29–31, 43, 49, 103, 109, 136, 141
oppression, 15, 97, 100, 130, 139, 153, 156, 158, 161, 163, 165, 178
optation, 178, 180

order, 52
organization, 25, 49, 179
organizing, 16–18, 25, 37, 40, 45–47, 51–53, 67, 93, 94, 139, 145, 164
orientation, 9, 15, 31, 110, 135, 137, 153, 155–157, 161
Orlando, 40
ostracism, 13
ostracization, 34, 173
other, 18, 30, 34, 36–38, 57, 65, 68, 125, 142, 145, 177, 187
outcome, 28
outlet, 68
outreach, 22, 112, 136, 141, 144
ownership, 52

pain, 15
panel, 110
parade, 45, 52, 53, 57, 138
part, 5, 15, 47
partiality, 118
participation, 95, 148, 172
partner, 65, 66
partnership, 36, 138
party, 111
passage, 24, 109, 110, 112
passing, 113–115, 170, 172
passion, 5, 16, 21, 23, 66, 89, 95, 108, 171
past, 149, 167
path, 3, 8, 14, 21, 25, 29, 36, 38, 60, 84, 91, 95, 105, 107, 114, 117, 172, 174
patience, 137
peer, 5, 8
people, 21, 29, 46, 52, 106, 130, 138, 139, 147, 156, 157, 167, 169, 170, 179, 185, 188

perception, 116, 125
performance, 179, 188
period, 5
periphery, 105
perseverance, 31, 105
persistence, 80
person, 5, 153, 161, 163
perspective, 22, 26, 90
phase, 5, 22, 29, 31
phenomenon, 145
photography, 179
piece, 115
pivot, 15
place, 9, 70, 110
planning, 52, 57, 138
platform, 9, 15, 25, 27, 46, 104, 106, 140, 142, 166, 167, 169, 180, 184, 187
play, 8, 29, 47, 55, 70, 88, 166, 167
plethora, 103
point, 13, 18, 23, 95, 174, 178
polarization, 111
policy, 23, 31, 115, 116, 128, 138, 164
pop, 183
population, 51
position, 29
potential, 25, 26, 49, 51, 52, 57, 58, 107, 111, 113, 122, 128, 130, 132, 144, 149, 170–172, 178, 183, 184, 187
poverty, 57, 156
power, 5, 9, 15, 16, 18, 23, 24, 26, 28, 31, 37, 38, 49, 53, 69, 70, 84, 100, 101, 105, 106, 110, 111, 115, 127, 128, 137, 139, 142, 151, 163, 173, 174, 177, 180, 189

practice, 16, 68, 139
prejudice, 45–47, 136, 137
presence, 111
present, 29, 54, 122, 168
pressure, 90, 98
prevalence, 87, 148, 185
prevention, 90
prey, 116
Pride, 52
pride, 10, 40, 52, 173, 183, 184, 188
principle, 78
privilege, 21, 26, 31, 139, 153, 161
process, 3, 45, 49, 52, 68, 85, 104, 106, 115, 172, 174, 187
product, 9, 127
production, 187
professional, 66, 68
profile, 118
profit, 167
program, 168, 170
progress, 29, 40, 47, 49, 58, 62, 81, 138, 165, 166, 172, 174, 180
prominence, 24, 26, 98
promotion, 73
protection, 23
protest, 17, 18, 45, 57
public, 26, 37, 45, 48, 52, 67, 109–112, 116, 125, 145, 171, 179, 186, 188
punk, 188
purpose, 45, 167, 174
pursuit, 50, 61, 64, 68, 84, 89, 111, 132, 151
push, 112
pushback, 57, 60

quality, 25, 156

queer, 4, 5, 8, 21, 22, 24, 30, 53, 61, 82, 153, 161, 163, 183–185, 188
quest, 8, 36, 42, 97, 128, 174
quo, 18, 29, 56, 105, 107, 120, 139, 155, 171, 183

race, 15, 31, 47, 128, 138, 153, 155–158, 161, 163
racism, 45, 156
radio, 52
rally, 53
rallying, 178, 183
range, 121, 138, 186
reach, 13, 26, 42, 52, 84, 128, 142, 147, 186
reaction, 53, 61
reality, 22, 51, 97, 168
realization, 5, 9, 12, 58, 103
realm, 122, 133, 135, 151, 153, 170, 182, 187
recognition, 18, 21, 23–26, 31, 97, 120, 157, 165–167
recovery, 90, 91
reflection, 47, 68, 113, 174
reframing, 45, 48, 50
refusal, 17
region, 88, 172
rejection, 43, 157
relationship, 65, 66, 94, 95, 169
relief, 95
reluctance, 103
reminder, 29, 40, 53, 107, 165, 174
report, 4, 156, 157
representation, 13, 29, 37, 53, 73, 105, 107, 110, 116, 119–121, 128, 148, 154, 164, 179, 182, 184–187
repression, 80

reputation, 8, 26
research, 58
resentment, 174
resilience, 5, 9, 13, 14, 18, 19, 21, 24, 26, 28, 30, 31, 39, 40, 42, 43, 45, 48, 49, 51, 60, 70, 80, 90, 91, 97, 100–102, 107, 115, 136, 144, 166, 168, 174
resistance, 4, 15, 17, 26, 29, 56, 70, 80, 88, 107, 135, 136, 138, 173, 178, 180, 184, 188
resolution, 95, 124
resolve, 29, 45, 110
resonance, 178
resource, 130
respect, 47, 84, 120, 135, 136
respite, 68
response, 8, 45, 60, 84, 97, 179
responsibility, 103, 169
result, 67
retaliatory, 95
retribution, 95, 97
revolution, 21
richness, 71, 120
ridicule, 45
rift, 93
right, 21, 110, 154
rise, 24, 26, 38, 98, 121, 144, 145, 171
risk, 167, 178, 179
road, 173
role, 8, 16, 25, 26, 29, 36, 38, 47, 55, 61, 70, 89, 95, 117, 125, 144, 157, 166–168, 171, 178, 179, 187, 188
romance, 70
room, 24
routine, 68

Index 207

safety, 53
sanctity, 56
sanctuary, 9
Saul Alinsky, 16
scale, 25, 40, 78, 89, 167
scarcity, 69
scenario, 94
scene, 185
scholar, 161
school, 5, 8, 13, 15, 27–30, 168, 171, 173
scope, 81, 185
scripture, 135
seat, 103
section, 31, 36, 40, 56, 64, 69, 71, 74, 77, 80, 87, 93, 95, 100, 108, 111, 113, 116, 117, 120, 122, 125, 128, 130, 133, 137, 140, 142, 147, 155, 158, 163, 165, 168, 170, 173, 178, 180, 187
self, 3, 5, 7, 8, 48, 66, 68, 90, 91, 145, 173, 174, 178, 183
sense, 4, 16, 17, 36, 37, 45, 48, 52, 68, 69, 85, 88, 97, 105, 138, 139, 142, 157, 166, 169, 170, 174, 186
sentiment, 88
series, 16, 47, 52, 117
service, 57, 169
set, 68, 98, 116, 135
setting, 8, 68
severity, 145
sex, 23, 87, 135, 141
sexuality, 3, 29, 31, 56, 131, 183
shape, 16, 26, 30, 116, 158, 161, 184
share, 8, 22, 29, 37, 46, 47, 49, 57, 85, 88, 95, 111, 117, 121, 135, 141, 142, 144, 147, 149, 169, 171, 186, 187
sharing, 9, 23, 38, 70, 84–87, 97, 117, 130, 136, 174
shift, 48, 57, 90, 105, 136
shooting, 40
sign, 91
signage, 138
significance, 47, 52, 53, 69, 70, 74, 113, 133, 158, 165, 170
silence, 148
sin, 57
site, 178
skepticism, 29
skill, 124, 170, 171
socializing, 68, 95
society, 3, 7, 21, 23, 30, 40, 43, 45, 47, 51, 53, 54, 56, 58, 69, 76, 87, 105, 115–117, 120, 121, 125, 130, 137, 154, 157, 160, 162, 179, 180, 182, 189
socio, 31
sociologist, 15
solace, 65, 95
solidarity, 13, 14, 19, 31, 40, 47, 48, 55, 61, 80, 82, 84, 85, 88, 97, 100, 130, 137, 139, 141, 160, 166, 169, 180, 183, 184, 186
song, 183
soundtrack, 188
source, 8, 89, 95
South Africa, 179
space, 14, 47, 49, 141, 142, 147, 168
spark, 38
speaker, 13
speaking, 171

spectrum, 52, 106, 138, 165, 171, 185, 187
speech, 18, 28, 40, 42, 53, 141, 143, 146, 148
sphere, 103
spirit, 37, 53, 64, 90, 97, 174
spokesperson, 25
spread, 17, 52, 87, 141, 143
square, 53
stage, 37
stake, 14, 109
stance, 135
stand, 14, 16, 40, 45, 55, 97, 117
state, 58
statement, 24, 26, 51, 103, 154
statistic, 22
status, 15, 18, 29, 31, 47, 56, 105, 107, 120, 138, 139, 153, 155, 171, 183
step, 31, 37, 52, 53, 58, 115, 155, 171
stereotype, 117
stigma, 15, 34, 69, 80, 90, 156, 173, 188
stigmatization, 116
Stonewall, 157, 166
story, 9, 13, 26, 45, 117
storytelling, 9, 70
strain, 93, 95, 97
strategy, 22, 49, 56, 68, 106, 111, 117, 128, 130, 135
stratification, 161
strength, 30, 49, 71, 89, 97, 99–102, 163
stress, 68, 71, 94
struggle, 3, 13, 15, 16, 21, 23, 42, 52, 66, 68, 70, 82, 84, 89, 90, 100, 111, 113, 115, 139, 173, 175, 180

student, 15, 37
study, 9, 156
substance, 156
success, 16, 26, 35, 45, 49, 53, 58, 87, 97, 99, 100, 105, 130, 165, 171
summary, 16, 26, 31
support, 7–9, 14, 24, 26, 28, 30, 38, 40, 45–51, 57, 60, 68, 73–76, 90, 91, 94, 95, 97, 99–102, 109, 110, 116, 125, 136, 138–142, 144, 154, 167, 171, 178, 180, 185
surge, 109, 145
surveillance, 144
sustainability, 170
sway, 56, 110
system, 95, 110

table, 103
talent, 170
tapestry, 5, 15, 54, 69, 70, 103, 163, 187
task, 11
teacher, 8
team, 17, 37, 51–53
tech, 146
technique, 48
technology, 38, 84, 144, 146–149
teen, 5
tenacity, 36, 105
tension, 29, 49
term, 21, 84, 161, 163
test, 29
testament, 16, 24, 28, 31, 97, 115, 174
the United States, 116, 136
theater, 182–184

Index

Theodor Adorno, 182
theory, 16, 21, 48, 61, 71, 80, 82, 108, 111, 124, 128, 130, 153, 158, 161, 165, 166, 178, 182
therapy, 48
Thompson, 8
thought, 182
thread, 54
threat, 13, 17, 23, 25, 29
time, 16, 24, 40, 66–68, 94, 146, 147
tokenism, 185
toll, 48, 90, 93, 95
tomorrow, 168, 170
tool, 113, 132, 140, 142, 147, 165, 178–180, 186–189
topic, 8
torch, 170, 172
totality, 156
town, 112
tradition, 51, 105, 108
traditionalist, 29
tragedy, 40
training, 47
trait, 43
transfer, 84, 170
transformation, 132, 173, 174
transgender, 46, 47, 52, 130, 138, 147, 156–160, 164, 169, 172, 185, 188
transition, 10, 170, 172
transnationalism, 80
transphobia, 22, 45, 47, 53–56, 80–82, 87, 173
trepidation, 51
triumph, 13, 24, 137, 139
trust, 84
turn, 58, 122
turning, 18, 23, 174

underpinning, 31, 111
understanding, 5, 9, 13–16, 21, 22, 40, 45, 47, 49, 51, 53, 57, 58, 65, 66, 69, 70, 76, 80, 88, 110, 117, 119, 120, 122, 124, 128, 130, 133–135, 137–139, 145, 151, 153, 154, 157, 161, 174, 179, 182, 186, 187
unity, 18, 26, 28, 36, 45, 60, 104, 130, 137–139, 142
up, 3, 7, 17, 28, 40, 138
uprising, 157
use, 38, 117, 125, 145, 178, 179
utilization, 149

validation, 8, 9, 95, 165
vehicle, 182, 187
Vex, 3–5, 7–9, 11, 13–18, 21–26, 28–30, 35–38, 40, 46–49, 53, 56, 57, 59, 60, 63, 66–68, 84, 87–91, 93–95, 97–100, 104–110, 128, 145, 146, 153, 170–174
Vex Aleron, 3, 5, 7, 10, 14, 16, 21, 24, 26, 29, 36, 38, 40, 42, 45, 47, 48, 51, 54, 56, 58, 61, 64, 66, 68, 73, 80–82, 84, 87, 89, 91, 93, 95, 97, 98, 103, 105, 108, 115, 117, 125, 145, 153, 155, 168, 170–172, 175
Vex Aleron's, 18, 26, 31, 49, 63, 84, 89, 97, 105, 107, 111, 172, 174
victory, 24, 105, 115
video, 52
view, 56
vigilance, 47

violence, 38, 40, 87, 97, 164, 179
visibility, 18, 24, 30, 34, 36, 38, 51–53, 56, 69, 117, 120, 128, 130, 142, 167, 179, 183–185, 188
vision, 29, 36, 51, 137
voice, 26, 30, 108, 132, 169
vote, 23, 24, 110
vulnerability, 156, 174

warrior, 66
wash, 3
wave, 3, 84
way, 19, 36, 56, 84, 87, 107, 124, 137, 168, 172, 173, 182, 186, 187, 189
weakness, 91
web, 45
week, 36
welfare, 135, 136

well, 26, 45, 58, 70, 76, 90, 91, 145
whirlwind, 64, 66, 89
willingness, 34, 171
withdrawal, 94
woman, 156
word, 17, 52
work, 15, 22, 45, 47, 67, 68, 82, 87, 89, 139, 157, 167, 170, 179, 183, 185, 187, 188
workplace, 156
workshop, 40
world, 24, 69, 70, 77, 87, 93, 96, 99, 107, 166, 185, 186
writing, 8

yoga, 68
youth, 11, 13, 18, 22, 24, 26, 30, 36–38, 74–76, 168, 169, 183

Zanele Muholi, 179

Milton Keynes UK
Ingram Content Group UK Ltd.
UKHW020316021124
450424UK00013B/1283